create and display

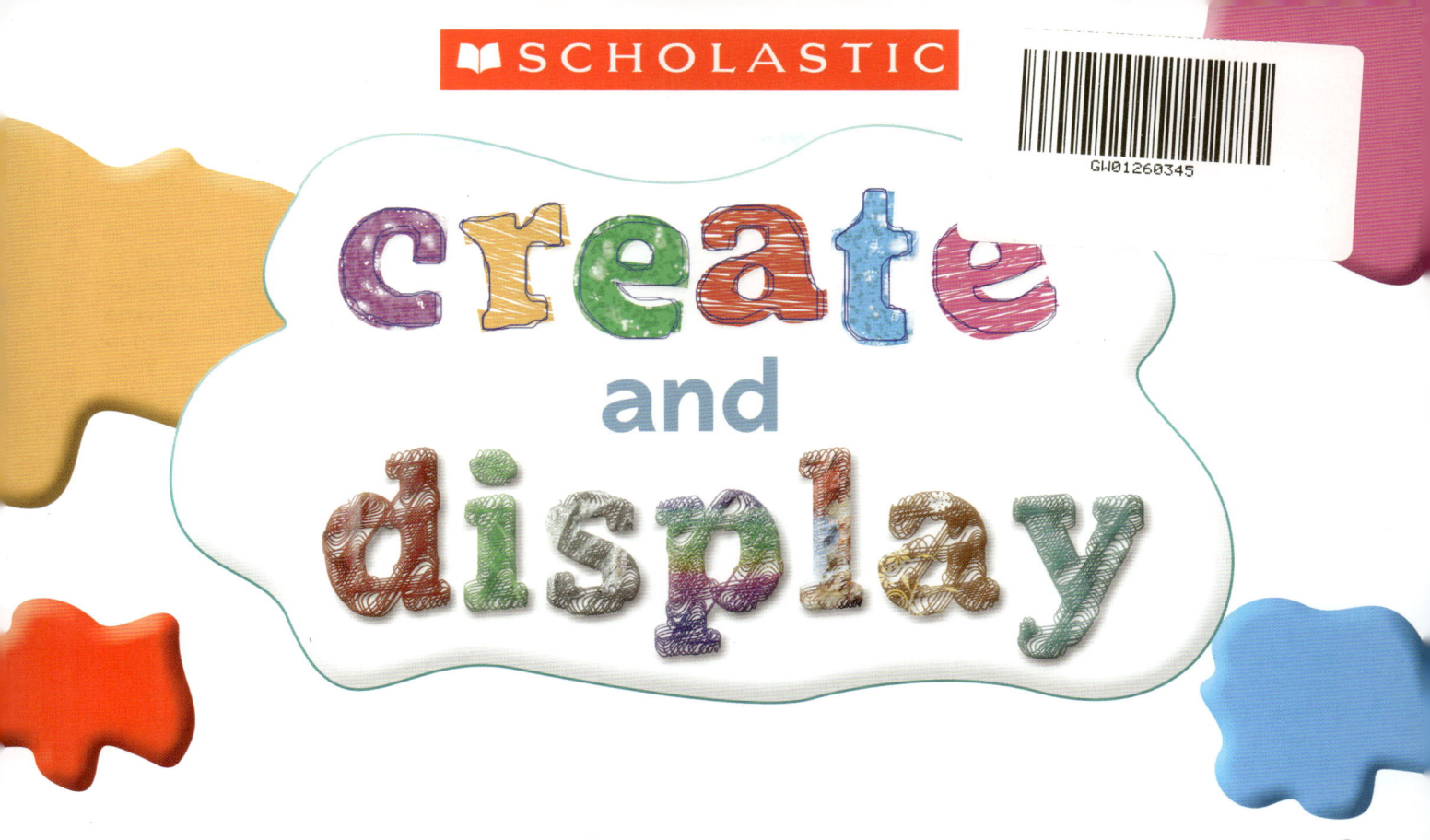

Nature and the Environment

Full of exciting activities and displays for the whole curriculum

Ages 4-11

Jean Evans

SCHOLASTIC

Book End, Range Road, Witney, Oxfordshire, OX29 0YD
www.scholastic.co.uk

© 2012, Scholastic Ltd

123456789 0123456789

British Library Cataloguing-in-Publication Data
A catalogue record for this book is available from the British Library.

ISBN 978-1407-12528-2
Printed by Bell & Bain Ltd, Glasgow

Text © 2012 Jean Evans

Jean Evans hereby asserts her moral rights to be identified as the author of this work in accordance with the Copyright, Designs and Patents Act 1988.

All rights reserved. This book is sold subject to the condition that it shall not, by way of trade or otherwise, be lent, hired out or otherwise circulated without the publisher's prior consent in any form of binding or cover other than that in which it is published and without a similar condition, including this condition, being imposed upon the subsequent purchaser.

No part of this publication may be reproduced, stored in a retrieval system, or transmitted, in any form or by any means, electronic, mechanical, photocopying, recording or otherwise, other than for the purposes described in the lessons in this book, without the prior permission of the publisher. This book remains in copyright, although permission is granted to copy pages where indicated for classroom distribution and use only in the school which has purchased the book, or by the teacher who has purchased the book, and in accordance with the CLA licensing agreement. Photocopying permission is given only for purchasers and not for borrowers of books from any lending service.

Due to the nature of the web we cannot guarantee the content or links of any site mentioned. We strongly recommend that teachers check websites before using them in the classroom.

Commissioning Editor
Paul Naish

Development Editor
Emily Jefferson

Editors
Fliss Bage and Simon Bage

Series Designer Andrea Lewis

Cover Design Sarah Garbett

Designer Sonja Bagley

Photography
Alan Sill and Gareth Boden

Acknowledgements

Jean Evans would like to thank several people for their important and inspiring contributions to the production of this book. Firstly, of course, the children and staff from Heathfield Primary School, Darlington, Tendring Primary School, Essex, Yarm at Raventhorpe Preparatory School, Darlington and Yarm School Nursery, Yarm, for their hard work, creative ideas and cooperation in producing the displays in the book, with a special mention going to the following teachers for their endless support and enthusiasm: Anne Clarke, Plum Harrison, Jenny Hill, and Rachel Jopling. Thanks also go to the Y1/2 children at Dodmire School, Darlington, for helping with individual artwork.

Jean is also grateful to Duncan Allen, outreach officer and project manager from Suffolk County Council Archaeological Service, who helped the children at Tendring Primary enormously with their work on rubbish; Alan Sill for his exceptionally good photographs; and in particular Paul Naish at Scholastic for his unerring support throughout the project.

Finally, a special thanks goes to Jean's daughter, Charlotte Spiers, for her positive encouragement and enthusiasm while trialling the activity ideas.

Images:

Page 6, Pine cones © Kamira/shutterstock, Feathers © Oculo/shutterstock; page 7, Prehistoric lizard of tyres © Malota/shutterstock; page 12, Leo Sewell's Junk Art Penguin © Barcroft Media/Getty Images; page 20, Happy Rizzi House, Braunschweig, Brunswick, Lower Saxony, Germany, Europe © imagebroker/Alamy; page 27, Tiger © Raimonds Bursch/istockphoto, Polar Bear © Michel de Nijs/istockphoto, Beaver © Kaj Wismar/istockphoto, African Elephant wading, Chobe River, Botswana © Liz Leyden/istockphoto, Koala © Craig Dingle/istockphoto; page 30, Offshore platform off the coast of Scotland © Yvan/shutterstock; page 55, Mount Everest © Grazyna Niedzieska/istockphoto; page 57, Sahara Desert © Giorgio Fochesato/istockphoto

All other images © Scholastic Ltd.

Contents

Introduction 4

Conservation and Planet Resources

At our Fingertips 6
Rubbish and Recycling 8
Celtic Roundhouse 10
Something from Nothing 12
The Sun and the Greenhouse Effect 14

The Local Environment

School Allotment 16
Where We Live 18
Up Your Street 20
My House 22

Conservation of Living Things

Underground, Overground 24
Going, Going, Gone 26
Down to Earth 28
Oil on Water 30

Natural Colours and Patterns

Colour Charts 32
Floral Impressions 34
Spirals and Curls 36
Tree Spirits 38
Webs of Wonder 40
Sunshine and Shadows 42
Day and Night 44
Patterns in Nature 46

Weather

Sudden Showers 48
Sing a Rainbow 50

Different Environments

Save the Rainforest 52
Mountains 54
Deserts 56
Cold Lands – the Poles 58
Cold Lands – Arctic Tundra 60

Energy

Fossil Fuels 62
Wind Power 64

Art Exhibition

Explosion of Feet 66
Pop Art 67
Line and Colour 68
Aztec Shields 69
Circles of Colour 70
Natural Silhouettes 71

create and display: Nature and the Environment

Introduction

Create and Display: Nature and the Environment aims to raise children's awareness of the world in which they live through a range of exciting practical, creative and display opportunities. There is an emphasis on conservation in that children are encouraged to recognise the importance of protecting those living things facing imminent danger from extinction and to look at ways of conserving our dwindling natural resources.

The Role of Display

Perhaps the most important role of a display is to provide children with a designated platform on which they can share their work and ideas with others. Individuals feel valued when they see that their work is included, and pairs, groups and whole classes of children learn the significance of teamwork. The benefit to self-esteem, along with the fostering of a sense of belonging arising from involvement in the creation of displays, is immeasurable.

Another feature of a good display is the potential for generating learning opportunities. Ideally, children's work should always be included, but there should also be a strong adult input in the form of printed labels, captions and informative materials to help put across the underlying educational focus of the display.

Inherent in any well-thought-out and well-executed display is the opportunity for children to develop their design and technology skills: for example, as they explore and experiment with ways of attaching or representing 3D objects on a 2D board. Mathematical skills will be needed when planning out designs, measuring materials and representing 3D shapes, and literacy and ICT skills will be enhanced with the creation of appropriate labels and captions. Opportunities to learn new creative techniques abound as children find ways to represent their ideas – often following examples from famous works of art – and put into practice skills such as collage, print, spatter, stipple and colour-mixing.

In this book, strong emphasis is given to the overall appearance of a display, with due consideration to colour, position, layout and borders. Rather than commercial border rolls, suggestions for different border techniques for children to try for themselves are given. This is cost-effective and adds further individuality to a display. Experimenting with borders encourages children to focus on how colour, design and pattern can link effectively with the overall theme for the display.

create and display: Nature and the Environment

Main Themes

The book is divided into eight chapters, each focusing on a specific theme. However, the individual spreads within these chapters can easily be linked with others from different chapters: for example, the work on allotments in 'School Allotment' (see Chapter 2) works well with the study of growth above and below ground in 'Underground, Overground' (see Chapter 3). Teachers can 'mix and match' to suit their particular planning and educational aims.

Discuss, Experiment, Display, Link

Each display topic has been divided into four main sections providing opportunities to:

Discuss
A 'Whole-class Starter' has been included to inspire and motivate children. This includes a discussion opportunity when a teacher can establish the level of previous knowledge on a subject and children can ask questions to ensure understanding of facts. Interesting props and resources are suggested to focus children's attention.

Experiment
'Practical Activities' for small-group and individual work encourage a 'hands-on' approach so that children can discover facts for themselves and so clarify their understanding of whole-class discussions. The creative and written work generated by these activities can be saved and used for displays.

Display
'Display Ideas' are given for introduction to children after exploring the topic fully through class discussion and practical activities. This section provides ideas for the creation of a main display, or small displays, to celebrate and promote the children's learning.

Link
'Cross-curricular Links' are included because when children learn through a meaningful experience it is seldom just knowledge of one curriculum subject that is enhanced, rather their learning overlaps into other subjects. In this book, although each spread is given a specific learning focus, this section provides suggestions as to how the spread theme can be linked to other curriculum areas.

Jean Evans

Chapter 1: Conservation and Planet Resources

At our Fingertips

Whole-class Starter

- Talk to the children about the idea of creating their own art and design area which they could visit in their free time, as well as during planned activity time, to explore and work with some of the recycled materials they have collected.
- Encourage them to consider what they think will be needed in terms of tools and equipment, furniture, materials, storage systems and display facilities. Jot down good ideas on a posting wall for reference.
  - Ask individuals to draw a plan of how they think the area should be organised, referring to the ideas on the posting wall. Come to a class agreement on the most suitable design.

Focus of Learning
To choose appropriate tools and techniques for a given task

create and display: Nature and the Environment

Chapter 1: **Conservation and Planet Resources**

Practical Activities

- Work with a small group of children to set up the structure of the area with the available storage units, tables and chairs in place. Try to leave a large space to work in with easy access to the recycled materials and mixed media.
- Consider how resources should be arranged for easy access: perhaps clear plastic jars along a shelf for storing fabric scraps sorted by colour, and floor bins for larger recycled materials such as cardboard and plastic tubes and boxes.
- Make silhouettes from sticky-backed coloured plastic on unit tops to store containers for brushes, pencils and different-shaped tools.
- Decide where finished artwork will be stored: for example, racks for paintings, and shelves or unit tops for 3D models.
- Store items such as scissors and tools safely in designated containers.
- Consider introducing a mobile version of your outdoor areas to extend possibilities for working with larger recycled materials, such as tyres and wire reels.
- Bring the class together regularly to discuss the area and to consider ways to modify and improve it.
- Visit a local tip or recycling centre to establish the sort of waste that can be recycled.
- Set up a class recycling centre and invite the children to bring in suitable items.

Display Ideas

- Introduce as many display boards and surfaces as space allows to celebrate group creations or individual works of art.
- Include labelling, notices and instructions with appropriate consistent lettering so that the children always know what to do with things and where to put them. Encourage the children to label their own work and add captions where appropriate. Create dual-language labels if applicable.
- Set up and display rules for returning equipment after use, replenishing resources and storing work tidily so that the area is always welcoming for the next child who visits.
- Change one of the display boards or unit tops regularly to follow a specific theme – for example, seasonal finds, action photographs, interesting objects collected on the beach or prints of work by a famous artist – in order to inspire the children to experiment with new ideas and directions.

Cross-curricular Links

- **Maths** – Create a storage system based on the shapes of the items available: for example, 'spheres', 'cylinders' and 'cubes'. Encourage the children to sort recycled paper and card by type, thickness, size, shape or colour.
- **Science** – Sort the recycled materials into different categories: for example, 'man-made' and 'natural'; 'wood', 'metal' and 'plastic'; 'rigid' and 'flexible'.

create and display: Nature and the Environment

Chapter 1: Conservation and Planet Resources

Rubbish and Recycling

Whole-class Starter

- Make a list of things that might be disposed of by a family today. Consider where this rubbish goes after it is collected from our homes or municipal tips.
- Do the same for a family of Celts or Victorians and ask the children what similarities and differences they notice.
- Encourage the children to consider how household waste might differ at different points in time, particularly times that link with their previous learning experiences: for example, in the Victorian and Celtic eras.

Practical Activities

- If possible, invite an artist/historian/archaeologist from the community to work with the children on rubbish through the ages.

Focus of Learning
**To examine methods of recycling household waste
To consider how household waste differs at different points in time**

- Bury objects resembling suitable items of rubbish from a particular period in history in a bucket: for example, pieces of pottery, metal objects or bones. Provide the children with trowels for excavation, a container for discarded soil, sieves for removing excess soil, trays to put their finds in and toothbrushes to clean them with.
- Create a portable display for the children to refer to, giving hints as to how to identify small finds.

create and display: Nature and the Environment

Chapter 1: **Conservation and Planet Resources**

- Emphasise the need to wash hands thoroughly after investigations.
- Divide the class into groups and provide each group with a bucket of buried rubbish to investigate. Engage them by inviting them to be detectives, trying to discover what sort of family disposed of the rubbish in their bucket. Encourage them to identify some of the items and ask who might have used them and when.
- Once all of the rubbish has been sorted, invite the groups in turn to say what they have discovered about their family.

- Consider how to categorise the artefacts: for example, by the material they are made of, their probable use and whether they are natural or man-made.
- Now discuss what we do with rubbish like this in modern times. Explore the children's knowledge of recycling – from household rubbish and sorting, to trips to the local tip. Bring in a collection of materials and sort them into various suitable categories.

Display Ideas

- **Recycling Display:** Make paper recycling 'bins' and attach all of your sorted material. Add labels to create an effective recycling display.
- **Archaeological Display:** Ask each child to draw an artefact and then write a paragraph about its probable origin underneath. Create a group display using photographs and the children's individual work linked to a particular bucket of rubbish.

- Allow time for free creative exploration: for example, working with chosen pieces of rubbish to create collage work, sculptures, models or prints. Display the finished work, along with captions.
- Create an interactive indoor display, using wall boards and tables, tracking the exploration process along a timeline, and displaying the children's photographs, written work and artwork.

Cross-curricular Links

- **Science** – Categorise rubbish according to materials or purpose: for example, bone, stone, pots and jewellery. Discuss which material preserve well and which do not.
- **Geography** – Identify some physical and human processes linked to managing waste and recycling.

create and display: Nature and the Environment

Chapter 1: **Conservation and Planet Resources**

Celtic Roundhouse

Creating an Ancient Learning Environment

- Develop relationships with local experts and professionals who have an interest in community education, such as archaeological outreach officers. The examples on these pages show how you can work with these experts in order to develop a project involving the whole school and the wider community.
- Creating environmentally themed structures, such as a Celtic roundhouse, a Roman pit kiln and vegetable garden, willow sculptures and a clay bread oven – connects children to their community, as well as helping them gain an understanding of their local historical environment.
- This exemplary approach can be adapted to suit location: for example, to investigate coastal features or particular historical sites.

Focus of Learning
To find out about how people lived in the local environment in Celtic times

Whole-class Starter

- Choose a topic related to the local environment, in this instance the changes in homes in the area over time.
- Invite the children to bring in photographs of homes in the locality and initiate discussion about the materials used to build them.
- Discuss who might have lived in the area in the past and what their homes might have looked like.
- Focus on the Celts and explore roundhouse images. Ask the children what we can find out about these houses from evidence available: for example, rain ditches and archaeological remains such as post holes and posts.

create and display: Nature and the Environment

Chapter 1: Conservation and Planet Resources

- Support understanding by making comparisons between these houses and the children's homes.
- If possible, introduce an artist/historian/archaeologist from the community to motivate the children as they try out their ideas for building a roundhouse.

Practical Activities

- Work with the children, and a community expert if applicable, to plan the house construction. Investigate materials used by the Celts and decide on the closest materials available today. Plan a construction sequence.
- During the construction, take photographs and notes to record progress. Be prepared to adapt plans should unforeseen difficulties arise, for example with weather conditions and supply of materials.
- Once the house is finished, discuss the building process and make links with the lifestyle of the Celts.
- Consider how the finished house and surrounding area can be used effectively to enhance learning: for example, reading stories in the house, whittling sticks and creating willow sculptures.

Display Ideas

- Create an indoor display showcasing the children's work: for example, weaving, paintings and written work. Arrange these among photographs showing the various stages of construction.
- Consider creating a temporary display of the children's 3D artwork, such as clay pots, weaving and willow sculptures, beside the roundhouse. Invite the children to explain to their parents how and why they made them.

- Encourage the children to display their own work individually: for example, arranging whittled sticks on a sheet of card.
- Focus on different aspects of roundhouse life and invite the children to create their own sections of a large indoor display: for example, 'Meals in the Roundhouse' or 'Sleeping in a Roundhouse'.

Cross-curricular Links

- **History** – Use the roundhouse for role play, comparing life in ancient times with life today.
- **PSHCE** – Sit in the roundhouse to discuss ways in which we pollute the environment today. Decide whether the same would apply to the original roundhouse dwellers.
- **Maths** – Ask the children to consider appropriate measurements for their house, for example the diameter and height. What factors will they have to take into account? For example, will the number of people living in the house affect the size?

create and display: Nature and the Environment

Chapter 1: **Conservation and Planet Resources**

Something from Nothing

Whole-class Starter

- Tip out an old sack of recycled materials, such as lollipop sticks, elastic bands, plastic bottle tops, broken toys (no sharp edges) and cardboard boxes, and explain that all of these items have been thrown away.
- Discuss what the children's families do with the items that they no longer need. Do they put them in the bin, visit the tip or find other ways of using them? Extend the discussion to consider why it is good to recycle.
- Explore some images of junk art and read any available blurb describing them. Talk about how the artists have used objects such as old cans, metal car parts and broken gadgets to

Focus of Learning

To use appropriate tools and techniques for their chosen task

create models, sometimes of specific things and sometimes as exciting abstract sculpture. Establish the meaning of 'abstract'.
- One artist you may like to investigate is Leo Sewell (1945–), an American artist who specialises in making sculptures out of junk. Visit his website **www.leosewell.net** where you can explore images of his work. He is best known for animal sculptures made from scrap metal, wood and plastic.

Chapter 1: **Conservation and Planet Resources**

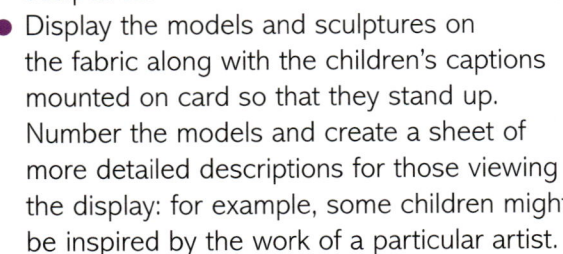

- Provide opportunities to create pictures using smaller pieces of recycled materials, such as paper and foil, that can be made into a collage on a thick sheet of cardboard.

Display Ideas

- Drape a clear surface, such as a cupboard or unit, in fabric ready to mount the children's 3D artwork. Choose colours according to the materials the children have used: for example, neutral for natural materials such as wood, or shiny silver fabric for metal sculptures.
- Display the models and sculptures on the fabric along with the children's captions mounted on card so that they stand up. Number the models and create a sheet of more detailed descriptions for those viewing the display: for example, some children might be inspired by the work of a particular artist.
- Display any 2D work – for example, a sweet-paper collage – on a display board backed with similar colour tones alongside or behind.
- Encourage the children to create sculptures on a large scale outdoors, for example using branches and other natural materials.

Cross-curricular Links

- **Science** – Create works of art by mounting different materials onto appropriate backing boards: for example, wood shavings and twigs on a wooden board, metal items on a foil plate, or fabric scraps on a carpet tile.
- **Maths** – Try creating symmetrical pictures, for example by using different-coloured bottle tops to make a butterfly collage.

Practical Activities

- Divide the class into groups and provide each group with a sack of recycled materials. Invite them to sort the items by the materials they are made from: for example, 'wood', 'metal', 'plastic' and 'mixed'.
- Provide paper, writing tools and a wide selection of joining materials, such as PVA glue, string, sticky tape, elastic bands and wire.
- Encourage the children to think of things they could make from their materials and to draw individual plans of this. Decide as a group which sculpture or model is to be made.
- Come together as a class and ask a spokesperson from each group to describe their work of art to the others.
- Ask the groups to write or type captions for their work.
- Rather than sort the materials beforehand, leave them in a big pile and let the children rummage through them to find items to use to create their own artwork.
- Suggest that the children follow a particular theme for their work, for example 'machines' or 'snails'.

create and display: Nature and the Environment

Chapter 1: **Conservation and Planet Resources**

The Sun and the Greenhouse Effect

Display board with sun collage titled "Our Sun" featuring facts:
- Greenhouses use solar radiation from the sun to warm plants.
- The planets travel around the sun.
- The sun is much bigger than the earth.
- The sun creates day and night and the seasons.
- The sun is spherical.
- We found out some hot sun facts.
- The sun is a star.
- Plants use the energy from the sun to produce sugar.
- Plants could not live without sunlight.

Whole-class Starter

- Explore some images of the Sun in space and talk about its appearance. Explain that you would like the children to discover interesting facts about the Sun and use these as part of a class display entitled 'Our Sun'.
- Pose questions for the children to consider. For example, *What is the Sun? Where is the Sun? How big is the Sun? Does the Sun move?* Talk about possible sources of information that the children might use for further research.
- Ensure the children understand they should never look directly at the Sun without suitable eye protection.

Focus of Learning
To learn more about the Sun and how it affects our lives

Practical Activities

- Discuss how the Sun is essential to life on Earth because without it the planet would be frozen and life would not exist. Talk about how heat, light and energy from the Sun help plants to grow. Introduce simple experiments to demonstrate this: for example, leaving some seedlings on a sunny window sill and putting others in a dark cupboard.
- Establish what the children know about 'global warming'.

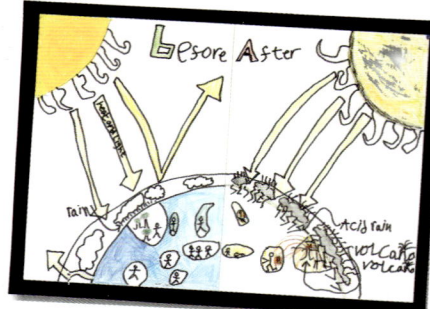

create and display: Nature and the Environment

Chapter 1: **Conservation and Planet Resources**

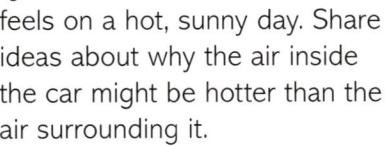

- Clarify what is meant by 'the greenhouse effect' by talking about how the inside of a car feels on a hot, sunny day. Share ideas about why the air inside the car might be hotter than the air surrounding it.
- Explain in simple terms that the inside of the car absorbs energy from the Sun and so it heats up. When the seats heat up they emit waves of energy but the glass in the car windows reflects some of them back again like a mirror and the car becomes hotter and hotter. Discuss how this principle might work to heat up a greenhouse.
- Extend this to illustrate what happens when solar energy reaches the Earth's atmosphere. Most of it passes into the atmosphere to heat up the Earth and then the excess heat is radiated back. However, harmful gases in the atmosphere prevent this excess heat from leaving and so the Earth's atmosphere gets warmer and warmer. Illustrate this with a simple diagram.
- Ask the children to consider how these harmful gases might be created, for example by car exhausts and waste from factories.
- Demonstrate how to help seedlings grow by using this greenhouse effect. Create greenhouses and cold frames using recycled clear plastic bottles and sheeting. Discuss practicalities such as joining the bottles together and fixing them to some sort of frame, or attaching plastic sheeting to a frame covering a wooden box.
- Invite the children to create their own group diagrams representing the greenhouse effect, showing the direction of the rays of energy using arrows, and annotating their diagrams with labels and captions.
- Finally, discuss what can be done to minimise the greenhouse effect on the Earth and ask the children to create posters demonstrating their ideas.

Display Ideas

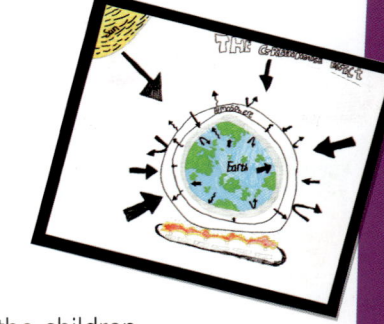

- Spread a large piece of strong paper on the floor and invite the class to sit around it. Discuss what the surface of the Sun might look like. Suggest to the children that they cover the surface of the paper in appropriate colours and textures to represent the Sun's surface, including features such as flames and hot spots. Provide a wide selection of paint and collage materials.
- Cut the completed surface into a large Sun shape and display it on a board, padding it underneath with newspaper and making the rays ripple to create a 3D effect.
- Print out the children's Sun facts, mount these on orange and red 'Sun spots' and attach them to the surface of the Sun with a hinge to create a 3D impression.
- Create a border by sponging red strips of paper with yellow and orange paint and attaching these in two alternating wavy lines around the display.
- Create displays using the children's diagrams demonstrating the damage caused by the greenhouse effect, and their posters depicting how the greenhouse effect can be minimised.

Cross-curricular Links

- **PSHCE** – Consider how we can protect ourselves from the dangerous rays of the Sun.
- **Maths** – Make comparisons of size, shape and distance between the Sun and the planets of the solar system while creating 3D models.

create and display: Nature and the Environment

15

Chapter 2: The Local Environment

School Allotment

Whole-class Starter

- Take the children on a tour of the school grounds and look at how the area is divided according to use: for example, playing games on hard and soft surfaces, growing things, providing shelter, nurturing wildlife.
- If there is already an allotment or vegetable plot, make a note of how it is arranged and what is growing there. If not, find a suitable place where this might be developed.
- Return to the classroom and ask the children to draw plans of the grounds, clearly marking the designated areas. Take turns to share completed plans with the rest of the class.

Practical Activities

- In the early spring, explain to the children that

Focus of Learning
To communicate specific information through plans and pictorial representations

you would like them to think about things that they might plant in the outdoor growing area. In the absence of such an area, dig over a small plot ready for planting.
- Make a list of possible vegetables, fruits and flowers that would be suitable to grow.
- Visit a garden centre to buy your chosen seeds. Take time to read or ask for brief instructions

16

create and display: Nature and the Environment

Chapter 2: The Local Environment

about planting times and reject any seeds on the list that are unsuitable.
- Plant the seeds and care for them according to instructions. Once the plants are established, discuss the importance of regular watering and weeding.
- With older children, experiment with growing techniques and new varieties of plants.
- Explain how some seeds and plants need to be protected from the cold and sudden changes in temperature. Look at actual cold frames and greenhouses or explore images in gardening catalogues. Talk about how these structures allow the heat from the Sun to pass through and then retain it.
- Create greenhouse structures by stringing together rows of empty clear plastic bottles and attaching them to a plastic tent frame.

Display Ideas

- Suggest that the children create a pictorial representation of their allotment or garden plot.
- Back a display board with hessian to represent the plot and create a border: for example, from empty seed packets or pictures of plants cut from seed catalogues.
- Invite the children to create individual rows of vegetables, each choosing a different variety from those already growing in the plot. Provide strips of brown paper to encourage them to create vegetables of a similar size and to place them in a row that will fit on the

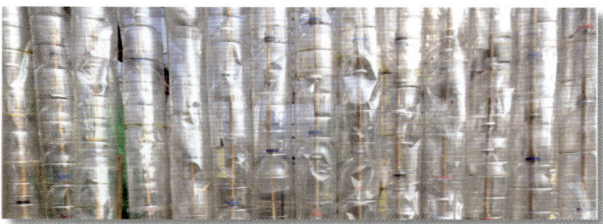

display. Provide a range of collage materials: for example, orange-tissue carrots with green-fabric tops, green-button peas and purple-cellophane beetroot.
- Arrange the completed rows of vegetables on the hessian to replicate your garden plot. Use wooden seed labels at the end of each row to name the vegetables.
- Using collage materials, add any other features of your allotment or garden plot: for example, a bubble wrap greenhouse or cold frames, collage compost heaps and raised beds, a black cardboard tube 'pipe' to a water butt, and tiny pebble paths.

Cross-curricular Links

- **Art and Design** – Make a miniature garden in a shallow bowl. Plant a grass lawn and add some tiny plants and moss. Introduce some model people and animals.
- **PSHCE** – Set up areas to encourage wildlife into your allotment or garden plot: for example, a bee nester or a bird-feeding station.

Chapter 2: The Local Environment

Where We Live

Exploring the Local Environment

- Begin this topic with a discussion about the area surrounding the school and invite the children to describe their journeys to school and back. Establish what familiar features the children see during these journeys.
    - Display a small-scale map of the area and ask the children to point out significant details, such as roads, rivers, railways, towns and villages.
    - Identify the location of the school and highlight this with a sticky note. Talk about where the school is located: for example, in the centre of a town or village, or in isolation along a country road.

Focus of Learning

To use maps to locate homes
To use creative techniques to represent homes and the local area

Whole-class Starter

- Explain that the focus of the lesson is to find out where the children live in relation to one another so that they can discover facts such as who has the shortest and who has the longest distance to travel.
- Ask what key fact each child will need to know in order to do this (their address).

18

create and display: Nature and the Environment

Chapter 2: The Local Environment

- Invite them to write their names on small pieces of paper. Spread the map on the floor and ask the children to place their names where they think they should be on the map. (Ensure that your chosen map is simple to read and encompasses all of the children's home locations.)

Practical Activities

- Ask the children to make a picture of their house using coloured sticky paper and card. Ensure that the finished houses are suitable for your planned display by providing pieces of card in appropriate sizes.
- Encourage the children to think about the shape of their houses and the number of windows and doors, but do not worry if all of the houses finish up as stereotypical images. The focus of the activity is on geographical skills and shape, and young children find creating regular houses quite a satisfying experience. They will still have freedom of colour choice to create their personal identity!
- Involve the children in typing small name cards to identify their houses.

Display Ideas

Creative representation

- Create a large pictorial map representing the area the children live in, beginning by marking in communication routes such as roads and railways before adding physical landmarks and buildings. Use a range of collage and print techniques.
- Hang the display at a low level so that the children can locate the position of their homes.

Map it out

- Hang a map of the area at child height and arrange the children's sticky-paper houses around it, involving the children in their choice of location: for example, deciding whether the houses of children who live in one village or town should be grouped together. Attach the name labels below the houses.
- Pose the question: *Do we really know who lives where from the display we have made?* Listen to the children's suggestions about how to make this more obvious and discuss how practical their ideas would be: for example, would address labels help?
- Introduce the idea of attaching a length of wool from each house to its location and try this out with a couple of examples, pausing to ask the children if they think this works before continuing.
- Discuss locations: for example, who lives nearest, who has the longest journey, which children are close neighbours.
- Display further work on the locality in adjacent spaces: for example, photographs of the children's homes and brochures about local landmarks.

Cross-curricular Links

- **Literacy** – Ask the children to describe to the class or write about their journey to and from school.
- **D&T** – Create a 3D version of your map on the floor to include model houses and buildings.

create and display: Nature and the Environment

Chapter 2: The Local Environment

Up Your Street

Preparation

- Provide the children with opportunities to explore how buildings on a street can be represented in unusual, often thought-provoking ways by different artists.
- Search for artists' images of buildings (Fazzino, Hundertwasser, Rizzi and Lowry are good examples) and show a selection to the children. Discuss how the artists have used colour, shape and pattern to create these exciting and often unusual impressions. Discuss how they differ from reality.

Whole-class Starter

- Explain that the focus of the lesson is to look at how one artist, in this example James Rizzi, creates images of streets of tall houses. Compare his pictures with 'normal' streets.
- Display one example of a Rizzi impression of a building alongside a photograph and make a list of similarities and differences in the two buildings: for example, the colours of the doors, windows and walls, the shape of the

Focus of Learning

To explore the work of an artist and use similar techniques to represent street buildings

roof, and additional features such as smiling faces and paintings of animals.
- Follow this by discussing what the children like and dislike about the images and whether they would change anything.

20

create and display: Nature and the Environment

Chapter 2: The Local Environment

- Explain that Rizzi sometimes paints brightly coloured designs on old buildings and show examples of this. Discuss whether this is a good idea and ask the children what they would paint onto these buildings.

Practical Activities

- Ensure that the children have access to the photographs and images talked about in the whole-class preliminary discussion before they begin to work in small groups.
- Provide four separate working areas:

1 Floor space with a long strip of blue paper so that the children can create a 2D street in the style of Rizzi.

2 An area with access to thin white or tracing paper, a range of brightly coloured pens and watercolour paints. The idea is to create pictures that can be mounted on glass so that the light shines through them.
3 A large area with a selection of suitable resources including recycled boxes, different types of paper (such as coloured tissue and sticky squares), black pens and joining materials (such as tape, elastic bands and glue). The aim is to create a 3D street of brightly coloured houses.
4 An area with easels, paints and paper. The aim here is to paint traditional houses.

- Ask the children to think about the way that Rizzi paints his houses and the shapes and colours he uses. Encourage the children to think 'out of the box' and to follow their own visual imagery.

Display Ideas

- Assemble the children's work into the four groups: the main group display of a street, houses influenced by Rizzi's work, 3D houses and paintings of traditional houses.
- Set up four displays, trying to be adventurous in your positioning: for example, choose a well-lit wall for the group display to emphasise reflections from windows, making good use of glass doors and windows for the Rizzi houses to encourage additional effects from the light flowing through them. Utilise corners for the 3D work to give the impression of a street corner and use odd sections of wall space to display traditional-house paintings.

Cross-curricular Links

- **Literacy** – Invite the children to create an image of an unusual house based on the above work and to invent a story about it. Encourage them to give the story an appropriate title, for example 'The House that Made Everyone Smile'.
- **D&T** – Using ideas from the pictures they have created, suggest to the children that they design a large house from recycled boxes and crates that they can use for role play. Provide brightly coloured paint to decorate the outside.

create and display: Nature and the Environment

Chapter 2: The Local Environment

My House

Whole-class Starter

- Invite the children to bring in photographs of their houses and discuss common as well as unique features.
- Make a list of the building materials used in the main construction of the children's houses under the headings 'walls', 'roof', 'windows' and 'doors'. Talk about why these materials are used and why, for example, a house could not be constructed entirely from bricks or glass.

Practical Activities

- Read or tell the story of 'The Three Little Pigs' and discuss the different materials used by the pigs to build their houses. Talk about the consequences of the pigs' choice of building materials and decide which house was strongest/weakest and why.
- Invite the children to make models of their houses using a range of suitable recycled materials, such as boxes, thick card and tubes. Provide safe joining materials to explore – for example, card strips, tape, PVA glue, paste, string, twist ties and elastic bands – and

Focus of Learning

To use creative and design techniques to represent their own homes in both two and three dimensions

encourage the children to experiment to find the best one for the task in hand.
- Provide paper, paint and mark-making materials so that the children can cover and decorate the houses if they wish to.
- Discuss the differences between a model and the real thing: *Why would it be difficult to use real building materials for their models?*
- Explore the inside of a doll's house and identify each room. Invite the children to make comparisons with the inside of their own houses. Explain how to draw a cutaway image of a house and encourage them to annotate cutaway pictures of their own houses.
- Encourage the children to create pictures of their houses from different textures: for example, by using collage materials to create the house and then taking a rubbing from it to form a textured image.

create and display: Nature and the Environment

Chapter 2: The Local Environment

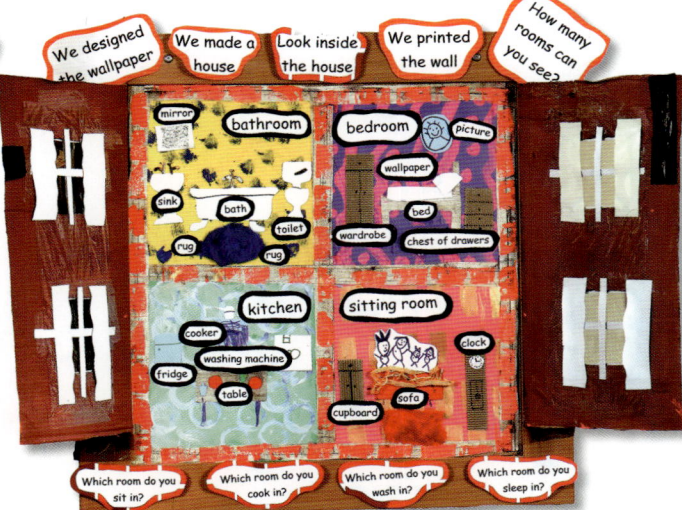

Display Ideas

- **Three Little Pigs:** Create a display relating to the story of the three pigs using a variety of techniques: for example, creating the houses from paper straws, lollipop sticks and brick-coloured rectangles.
- **Cutaway home:** Make a cutaway doll's house display by dividing a square board into four and cutting out four coloured pieces of paper to represent the rooms. Invite the children to print or draw designs on these to replicate wallpaper and attach these to the board.
- Create furniture, soft furnishings and appliances from collage materials and stick these in the relevant rooms.
- Make the outside of the house in the form of two doors made from thick card painted in a brick pattern. Tape them securely to the outside of the board and devise some sort of fastener so that they can be closed over the front of the house. The children can then open them to reveal the inside of the house.
- **Three dimensions:** Display the children's 3D models as a street or around a village green. Create stand-up labels identifying who lives in each house.
- **Using textures:** Display the children's textured houses on a large board backed with rubbings of bricks taken on an outside wall.

Cross-curricular Links

- **Literacy** – Invite the children to create small folding books to tell the story of a family living in their display doll's house. Ask them to act out the story using a real doll's house.
- **Geography** – Look at unusual houses around the world – for example, yurts, teepees, mud dwellings, tree houses and transportable nomad homes – and discuss why the building materials used are very different from each other.

create and display: Nature and the Environment

Chapter 3: Conservation of Living Things

Underground, Overground

Whole-class Starter

- Share the traditional stories 'The Enormous Turnip' and 'Jack and the Beanstalk'.
- Make comparisons: for example, between the size and shape of the turnip and the beans. Decide whether they grow under or over the ground.
- Divide a board into two sections headed 'Underground' and 'Overground'. Invite the children to write the names of vegetables

Focus of Learning

To name the main parts of a plant
To understand the importance of making healthy food choices

they know under the appropriate heading. Discuss the resulting list together, making any alterations necessary.

create and display: Nature and the Environment

Chapter 3: **Conservation of Living Things**

Practical Activities

- Provide the children with some vegetable seed packets to explore and decide which ones they would like to grow. Prepare a suitable plot, or obtain some large pots, and follow the instructions on the seed packets. Take particular note of when and where to plant the vegetables. Provide tools so that the children can be responsible for watering and weeding their growing plants.

- Follow the tried-and-tested method of growing broad beans, using a cut-down plastic bottle instead of a jar and compost instead of blotting paper. Make sure the beans are close to the side of the bottle so that the children can observe the growth of roots under the ground and shoots above.
- Grow onions in hyacinth jars and observe the roots growing down into the water below and the shoots stretching upwards.
- Grow potatoes in a bucket. When the main foliage begins to die, pull up the plant to reveal the tiny potatoes clinging to the roots.
- Invite the children to draw and label a diagram to show the parts of a plant.
- Create a set of laminated cards based on the labels in your display so that the children can read and match them.

Display Ideas

- Create a group display to show how vegetables grow under the ground.

- Create the backing using blue paper for above ground and hessian for below. Have fun adding texture to the hessian by thickening black, white and brown paint with PVA glue, sponging this all over and then sprinkling on sand and fine soil.
- Ask the children to choose vegetables that grow under the ground and decide how to make them using the recycled materials you have available: for example, an orange-fur carrot, a purple-crêpe-paper beetroot with added sweet wrappers, and tiny potatoes made from brown polystyrene packaging.
- Talk about how the vegetables might look above the ground by exploring web images, pictures and photographs, and then make stems and leaves from various recycled materials.
- Discuss the wildlife to be found over and under the ground and invite the children to choose their own materials to make tiny worms, brightly coloured birds and so on.
- Make labels for the display, defining them as 'under' or 'over' ground by mounting them on black or blue and then categorising them into words for living things, plant parts, environmental features such as 'sky' and 'clouds', and natural materials such as 'soil' and 'stones'.

Cross-curricular Links

- **Literacy** – Provide cameras, clipboards, magnifying glasses and writing materials so that the children can keep pictorial diaries of the growth of their vegetables.
- **Maths** – Encourage the use of mathematical language as the children name the vegetables that are 'under' and 'over' the ground and describe them using words such as 'long', 'short', 'straight', 'curved', 'wide', 'narrow', 'thick', 'thin' and 'tapering'.

create and display: **Nature and the Environment**

Chapter 3: **Conservation of Living Things**

Going, Going, Gone

Focus of Learning

To understand how species can become endangered or extinct

To learn about ways of saving endangered species

Whole-class Starter

- Show the children two pictures, one of an endangered animal, such as a polar bear, and another of an extinct creature, such as a dodo.
- Explain that one of them is already extinct but the other is in danger and likely to become so. Discuss the words 'extinct' and 'endangered' and come up with a class definition of each.
- Ask individuals to say which creature they think is the endangered/extinct one and to give reasons for their choice.

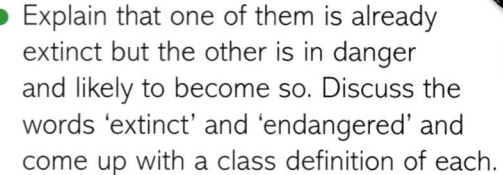

Practical Activities

- **Going, going, gone:** Divide the class into groups and ask half of them to search for facts about endangered creatures and the others to find out about extinct ones.
- Encourage the groups to note down interesting facts and then share their findings.
- Explain that you would like each group to create a large papier-mâché or fabric model of a chosen extinct or endangered creature set in an atmospheric landscape. Encourage them to make notes describing key facts about their chosen creature: for example, where it would live and what it would eat.
- Let the children make sketches of the proposed model and collect examples of the materials they plan to use. Ask the children to make a list of resources needed.
- Using their resource lists, invite the children to gather materials before starting to build their creatures. Provide somewhere to leave models during construction as this will probably take several sessions.

create and display: **Nature and the Environment**

Chapter 3: Conservation of Living Things

- Encourage the children to represent the concept of 'going, going, gone' in other ways, for example with clay models, drawings, paintings and poems.
- **Going local:** Encourage the children to become more aware of local endangered wildlife by researching local environmental organisations, for example projects aimed at supporting frogs, toads and newts.
- Set up a pond in your school grounds where creatures can thrive in an ideal safe environment.
- Introduce flowers and plants into your school grounds to support wild creatures such as butterflies and bees.
- Visit local wildlife centres and museums of natural history to further explore conservation.

- Create a suitable habitat area and arrange the models, with the endangered creatures to the left and the extinct creatures to the right.
- Hang the words 'Going, going, gone' along the back of the area.
- Make large labels showing the name of each creature and add some captions written or typed by the children.
- Have a table nearby for displaying the children's planning and research.

Display Ideas

- Invite the children to create a group display presenting their creatures in their natural habitats.
- Encourage the children to explore the form or shape of their chosen animal as they construct or create it.

Cross-curricular Links

- **History** – Discuss how scientists can learn about the size and shape of extinct creatures from fossils. Study fossils such as ammonites, ferns, shells and trilobites and make impressions of them in dough or clay.
- **Literacy** – Invite the children to make up poems about their creatures, or stories about events in their lives.

create and display: **Nature and the Environment**

Chapter 3: Conservation of Living Things

Down to Earth

Whole-class Starter

- Visit the school allotment or garden plot to look at compost heaps and bins. Alternatively, invite a keen gardener to talk about the value of composting as part of the regular cycle of growth and decay in the garden.
- Pass around a small bucket of compost for children to feel and smell. Ask: *What do you think that this compost was made from? Are any of the original ingredients recognisable? What has happened to them?*
- Introduce compost-related vocabulary, such as 'bin', 'heap', 'organic waste', 'rot' and 'decay', and establish meaning linked to facts the children remember from their own experiences.

Focus of Learning
To understand how organic waste can provide good nutrition for growing plants
To know what compost is and which materials can be used to make it

Practical Activities

- Extend the discussion about words associated with composting by asking children to write definitions for gardening terms, such as 'propagator' and 'organic liquid plant food'. Provide books, picture dictionaries and computer access to support the children.
- Read the appropriate section on composting from *Good Growing: A Kid's Guide to Green*

Chapter 3: Conservation of Living Things

Gardening (Klutz, 2011) and discuss what sort of waste materials the children think would be suitable to put in a compost bin.
- Suggest to the children that they get into groups to invent their own really exciting versions of compost by making up 'Marvellous Compost Stew' recipes.
- Compose a letter with the children's help asking parents to start composting and recycling, perhaps bringing in some organic waste for the school compost bins.
- Introduce some organic waste and encourage the children to experiment with ways of making their own mini composters. Watch what happens to your mini composters on the classroom window sill.

Display Ideas

- Recall the explorations and discussions related to composting and invite the children to create a large compost bin as the centrepiece of a display on composting. Make a list of suitable foods that could be put in this bin, and discuss why some suggestions would be unsuitable.
- Invite some groups to create collage items to go into the bin while others write up their recipes. Once the food items are finished, attach them inside a large outline of a compost bin made from coloured paper.
- Back a display board in sunshine yellow, discussing why this colour might be a good choice. Attach the compost bin collage to the centre and display the children's work around it: for example, some of their 'Marvellous Compost Stew' recipes, photographs and instructions for their mini compost maker, or 'Compost Vocabulary' lists.
- Create a title from large green lettering and a border, primarily green, from small pictures and a collage of fruits and vegetables.

Cross-curricular Links

- **PSHCE** – Consider the importance of composting when growing fresh fruits and vegetables as part of a healthy lifestyle. Discuss how composting waste, and using it to improve growth, can maintain sustainability in the environment.
- **History** – Invite elderly relatives to talk to the children about the importance of using gardens and allotments to cultivate fruit and vegetables during the Second World War when food supplies were scarce.

create and display: Nature and the Environment

Chapter 3: Conservation of Living Things

Oil on Water

Whole-class Starter

- Put some water in a clear bowl and invite a child to gently pour some drops of cooking oil onto it. Talk about what happens to the drops. Ask the children to try to mix the oil into the water and discuss what happens. Ask whether the oil has dissolved and establish that the oil and water remain separate.
- Talk about the different uses of oil, both commercial and domestic.

- Invite the children to share their knowledge about where oil comes from and look at images of oil rigs. Discuss how oil is transported by sea and explore images of oil tankers.
- Consider what might happen if some of this oil spills into the sea. Will it dissolve in the water? Read a news report and look at images of past oil spillages at sea, such as the BP oil spill in 2010, and discuss the impact on wildlife.

Focus of Learning
To understand the environmental effects of oil pollution

Practical Activities

- Put some oil and coloured water into a sealable plastic sandwich bag and seal it up. Pass this around and encourage the children to observe the patterns as the oil flows around giving a marbled appearance.
- Use dark-blue marbling inks to create images of oil floating on water. Fill a deep tray with water and gently drop the ink onto the water. Swish this around with a small stick. Slowly roll a sheet of paper over the surface and

create and display: Nature and the Environment

Chapter 3: **Conservation of Living Things**

We looked at The Deepwater Horizon oil spill (also referred to as the BP oil spill) which flowed for three months in 2010.

gradually peel it away to reveal the pattern on the paper.
- Encourage the children to experiment with different colours and colour combinations to create attractive patterns and then ask them to describe their pattern: for example, they may think it resembles a dragon or a magic creature.
- Look at images of birds that have been affected by oil spillages. What colour is the oil? Talk about how this will kill a bird gradually if not removed. Create a collage of a sad bird, using feathers, and dab these all over with black paint to represent the oil.
- Ask the children how they think conservation workers might remove the oil from birds. Try covering a soft toy bird with oil and washing it in water. Does this remove the oil? Now add some washing-up liquid or detergent to the water before washing the bird again. What happens is that the detergent creates an emulsion with the oil and water. Explain that this is how birds are cleaned by conservation workers.

Display Ideas

- Invite the children to create a group display about 'Oil on Water'. Mount the board with blue paper to represent the sea and create a border and title letters from strips of the children's marbling experiments.
- Think of a name for your collaged oil-covered bird, such as 'Pete the Pelican', then add a caption about how he is suffering.
- Surround 'Pete' with associated artwork: for example, the children's marbling and feather pictures, and any relevant resources such as oil- and water-filled toys, and bags of oil mixtures.

Cross-curricular Links

- **Literacy** – Have fun sending secret messages to one another using paper and oil. Using a thin paintbrush, write a message in oil on some paper. When the paper is dry, lift it up to the light and read the message.
- **Art and Design** – Half-fill some small recycled plastic bottles with water and a few drops of food colouring. Add some cooking oil and screw the lid back on. Shake the bottle to create attractive patterns and light effects. Try adding glitter, sequins and small objects to enhance these effects.

31

create and display: **Nature and the Environment**

Chapter 4: Natural Colours and Patterns

Colour Charts
Colours in Nature

Whole-class Starter

- Go for a walk in a natural environment, such as a wood or meadow, and ask the children to observe the colours around them. Explain that you want them to focus on the colours of nature rather than on man-made things such as signs and metal gates.
- Find a suitable place to sit and discuss the colours the children have noticed. Was there one predominant colour?
- Take cameras so that the children can record their discoveries.

Focus of Learning
To recognise colour in the natural environment

create and display: Nature and the Environment

Chapter 4: Natural Colours and Patterns

Practical Activities

- Pass around some paint colour charts from a DIY store and discuss how colours can have many shades. Talk about shades of colour the children might have noticed on their walk, for example red leaves and pink petals.
- Repeat your initial walk, this time asking the children to work in groups to collect examples of different colours to bring back to the classroom.
- Return to the classroom and ask each group to arrange their finds on a table. Provide them with paint charts so that they can match the items against the nearest colour shade: for example, most leaves, grass and mosses would match different shades on a green colour chart.
- Once the children have matched their finds to colours on the charts, suggest that they create their own versions of a paint chart to show the range of natural colours in the environment they visited.
- Provide thick card in colours suitable for all of the items the children have found and the paint charts already used. Ask the children to stick an appropriate paint chart to each sheet of card.
- Glue the natural finds, such as plant stems, flower petals and leaves, to the card alongside the paint chart: for example, a 'green' chart could have squares of shredded leaves, grass, stems and moss, while 'brown' could have twigs, bark and dead leaves.
- Obviously finds will be seasonal, so repeat this activity at different times of the year.
- Extend the charts by adding natural materials, for example hessian, wool, soil, sand and wood offcuts.
- With the same coloured card that the children used for their charts, and any finds that are left over, create free collage pictures in shades of one colour.
- Explore colour variations in fruits, vegetables and flowers, and invite the children to paint pictures of them. Match the colours and shades closely by mixing different amounts of primary colours and white paint.

Display Ideas

- Back a display board in a natural material, such as hessian, and display the children's completed charts on this.
- Add suitable labels and captions decided by the children, and create the title, 'Colours in Nature', using paper in natural shades.
- The children's free collage work can either be hung around the display or displayed separately.
- Ideally, these displays should be situated near an investigation table or in a creative area to stimulate the children's awareness of colours in nature.

Cross-curricular Links

- **Maths** – Sort seeds – such as sunflowers, rice and peas – according to colour and use PVA glue to attach these to coloured card to form interesting colour patterns in swirls and circles. (Check for allergies first.)
- **Literacy** – Encourage the children to use new and adventurous vocabulary when describing shades of colour, for example 'lime', 'mint', 'olive', 'pea', 'sage', 'sea' and 'emerald' green.

create and display: Nature and the Environment

Chapter 4: Natural Colours and Patterns

Floral Impressions

Whole-class Starter

- Provide the children with some poppies or sunflowers to explore and identify their key features, such as size, colour and shape of stalk, leaves and petals.
- Hand out photographs of the chosen flowers and ask the children to point out the features already identified.
- Show the children an appropriate floral print

Focus of Learning

To explore the work of famous artists and try out some of their techniques

by a famous artist: for example, van Gogh's *Sunflowers* or Monet's *Poppies*.
- Introduce the term 'artistic impression' and discuss what this means with reference

create and display: Nature and the Environment

Chapter 4: **Natural Colours and Patterns**

to the flowers and the works of art. Make comparisons between the artistic impression and the photographs. Which medium gives the most accurate representation? Ask which representation the children prefer and why.

Practical Activities

- Hand out smaller versions of the prints for pairs of children to share and invite them to write down appropriate words to describe the artists' work.
- Provide a range of creative materials, such as paint, collage materials, fabric scraps and coloured paper. Ask the children to create their own 'artistic impressions' of the flowers.
- Discuss ways of representing the flowers: for example, with thumbprints or paint spatter. Encourage lots of experimentation. Talk about the importance of light to artists and set up opportunities to work outdoors as well as indoors, on the ground, tables or easels. Demonstrate alternative techniques, such as combing thick paint mixed with paste to give textured effects, using fabrics and painting on wood or stones.
- Add an extra dimension to the work by involving local artists and family members, or by collecting a variety of waste resources from businesses.

Display Ideas

- Set up a display in a suitable place so that the children can take their families to see it. An entrance area or corridor is ideal.
- Consider the importance of the background and border for a wall display: for example, enhance a 'Poppies' display by using a red velvet background surrounded by borders of poppies made from strips of black paper painted with rows of red thumbprint 'poppies' with green painted stems.
- Alternatively, attach individual works of art to a supporting structure. A garden trellis is ideal as it provides additional scope for enhancement: for example, by threading green strips of ribbon, fabric and paper through the trellis around the children's work.
- Demonstrate various framing techniques for the children to try out: for example, double-mounting in contrasting coloured paper, or using hessian or thick card.
- Add to the attraction of the display by placing interesting artefacts on a table draped in colourful fabric: for example, a vase of flowers, artificial flowers to handle, magnifying glasses, books about flowers to explore and prints of linked works of art.
- Set up an art exhibition to showcase some of the work by the artists and the children.

Cross-curricular Links

- **Maths** – Look for patterns and shapes in real flowers and in their 2D and 3D representations.
- **Literacy** – Encourage the children to identify letters written on card petals and then arrange them to form 'word flowers'.
- **ICT** – Ask the children to work in pairs, looking in books and on suitable websites to find facts about the lives and work of different artists. Type and print out some of the relevant facts or save them on a CD-ROM.

create and display: **Nature and the Environment**

Chapter 4: Natural Colours and Patterns

Spirals and Curls

Whole-class Starter

- Show the children an image of *The Snail* (1953) by Henri Matisse (1869–1954) and ask them to describe what they see. Focus on the squares, their colours and the way they are placed in relation to one another. Look closely at how the artist has made them overlap and explain that seeing the shell of a snail inspired Matisse to recreate this design with roughly cut pieces of paper.
- Look closely at a real snail and discuss the shape, introducing the word 'spiral' to describe the shell. Does the work by Matisse look like a snail with a spiral shell?
- Talk about the way that a snail shell curls around and ask the children to think of other living things that have spirals and curls, such as a knot in a tree.

Practical Activities

- Invite the children to try ordering and overlapping squares made from different materials, such as felt, sticky paper or coloured card, to create their own small snail pictures.
- Use thick pens to draw spirals along strips of coloured paper.
- As you observe a snail together, discuss the slimy trail it leaves and ask the children to think of adjectives to describe the snail, such as 'gooey', 'slimy', 'hard shell' and 'waving eyes'. Talk about how the slimy trail is quite shiny and provide some silver paint so that the children can write their adjectives in 'slime' using a fine paintbrush.
- Go outside to look around for examples of spirals and curls in nature, for example the tendrils on a pea plant as they curl around a cane or fence to support the growing plant. Plant some bean seeds and watch them uncurl as the root begins to move downwards and the stem grows upwards.
- Glue some string in a spiral onto a small block of wood using PVA glue and use this as a

Focus of Learning
To create patterns and shapes with spirals and curls

create and display: Nature and the Environment

36

Chapter 4: **Natural Colours and Patterns**

printing block to create repeat spiral patterns or snail images.
- Attach string around a paint roller in a wavy fashion and use this to roll paint in curly lines along some paper.
- Cut out paper spirals, hang them up as mobiles and watch them curl and twist in the breeze.

Display Ideas

- Back a display board in blue to represent the sky above the habitat of a snail. Create a huge snail shape which will cover most of the display, cutting out a foot and head and then attaching these to the snail shell. Encourage the children to choose contrasting colours for this. Draw the spiral shape on the shell with a long curly line. 
- Glue the children's small 'Matisse' snails made earlier in a spiral pattern onto the snail shell, following the curly lines you have drawn.
- Embellish the snail with a cheeky grin and cover it with curly lines drawn by the children.
- Add some strips of green tissue to represent the grass the snail is sliding through.
- Make a border using the strips of coloured paper the children printed or drew their spirals and curls on.
- Attach the children's 'slimy trail' words to the display.
- Using patterned paper, cut out large letters to make the words 'spirals and curls' and arrange these in a clockwise direction on the edge of the snail shell so that the children discover a curly line as they read it.

Cross-curricular Links

- **Science** – Create model snails using clay, emphasising the spiral of the shell by making this separately and attaching it to the snail's body. Investigate snails and other molluscs.
- **PE** – Encourage the children to use a variety of body movements to recreate spirals and curls: for example, lying on the ground with arched back and curled-up legs, or twisting their arms in moving spirals.

create and display: **Nature and the Environment**

Chapter 4: Natural Colours and Patterns

Tree Spirits

Whole-class Starter

- Choose an atmospheric place, such as the centre of a woodland area or an outdoor story hut, to read *The Green Man* by Bel Mooney (Barefoot Books, 1997). Speculate on who this strange green man might be.
- Introduce the children to the legend of the Green Man, one of Europe's most ancient gods. Explain how he represents the forces of the natural world and reminds us of our role as caretakers of that world. Extend the discussion to include the wider notion of 'tree spirits' and consider the idea that these spirits are eager to share their profound knowledge of ways to care for the planet, particularly the forests and woods and the wildlife within them.

Focus of Learning

To use creative techniques and natural materials to represent characters from stories and from their own imaginations

38

create and display: Nature and the Environment

Chapter 4: Natural Colours and Patterns

- Discuss with the children how they might use natural materials to create their own representations of the Green Man, or indeed the tree spirits they see within their own imaginations, to watch over their woodland area or school grounds.

Practical Activities

- Working outdoors if possible, provide the children with clay to form the heads of their tree spirits. Encourage them to make these unique by shaping quirky facial features.
- Search for a range of naturally found materials to add interest to these features – for example, acorn eyes, leafy eyebrows and twiggy teeth – pushing them deep into the damp clay to secure them.
- While the heads are still damp, invite the children to decide upon the best locations for their tree spirits. Encourage innovative ideas, such as pressing the faces into the bark of a tree or sticking them to the surface of a log.
- Alternatively, wash thick card in green paint and attach natural materials to this to create the faces of tree spirits. Finish individual pictures with a unique border made from the same materials.
- Encourage the children to explore the idea of tree spirits through role play, drama and related stories by providing them with a range of green and brown textured fabrics to use as drapes and costumes. Suggest that they use found materials such as twigs and leaves to create headdresses and embellish costumes.

Display Ideas

- Suggest to the children that they create a display of their clay tree spirits on a tree, discussing the role the background will play in emphasising the idea that the trees and undergrowth are an integral part of the display.  
- Suggest creating a trail through the woodland to the display so that the uniqueness of the tree spirits can be enjoyed *in situ*. Work together to produce an A4 sheet with a dotted line marked with arrows to indicate the direction of the trail from 'start' to 'finish'.
- Talk about how art exhibitions often identify individual works of art with the title, name of the artist and a short blurb. Discuss whether attaching laminated captions to the tree spirits in this display would enhance or spoil the visual effect. Consider alternatives – a discreet laminated numbering system would work well together with an accompanying sheet.
- Create an indoor display using the card spirit faces created from natural materials. Invite the children to write their own captions about their chosen spirit.

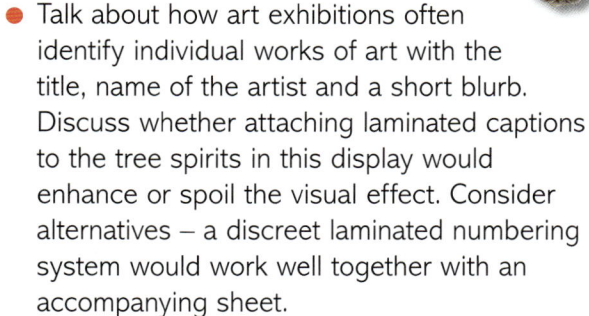

Cross-curricular Links

- **PSHCE** – Before making the spirits, consider the importance of using only found materials in order to preserve the natural environment.
- **Science** – Identify the trees in the woodland and discuss their similarities and differences before creating the spirits so that the children can attach their clay faces to a particular tree.

create and display: Nature and the Environment

Chapter 4: Natural Colours and Patterns

Webs of Wonder

Whole-class Starter

- Take the children outdoors on a hunt for spiders and their webs. Provide them with magnifying glasses, cameras and writing materials so that they can record their observations in detail without disturbing any spiders or other wildlife.
- Return to the classroom to talk about the discoveries the children have made: for example, the appearance of a spider, how many legs it has, where the webs were located and what they looked like.

Focus of Learning

To explore spiders' web patterns and recreate these using different creative techniques

Practical Activities

- Print the children's photographs and encourage them to explore these in groups, along with their own drawings and website and book images, to establish facts about spiders and their webs. Help them to compile the facts into books or ring binders.

create and display: Nature and the Environment

Chapter 4: Natural Colours and Patterns

central stick. Thread wool around and across the sticks to form the web.
- Thread ribbon in and out of the spokes of a wheel to resemble a web.
- The children might decide to develop the use of handprints and buttons in other ways: for example, to decorate white tiles or create colourful textured pictures on canvas.

Display Ideas

- Back a display board in a bright colour to contrast with the black and silver webs. Attach the children's webs made from buttons and thread on card.
- Provide some blue card circles and invite the children to drip silver paint onto them to form web-like lines and then glue their spider handprints to these. Attach them to the display between the button webs.
- Spread some strands of fine gossamer-like fabric over parts of the display to add to the web effect.
- Create a border using the spider handprints and buttons glued to strips of coloured paper. Add the title 'Webs of Wonder' from letters cut from web-patterned paper.
- Stand a bare branch in a pot in front of the display and drape this in gossamer-like threads. Include some model spiders scuttling among them.
- Display any children's related artwork around the display, such as canvas pictures, or tiles decorated with handprints and buttons and glazed with PVA glue.

Cross-curricular Links

- **PSHCE** – Discuss how some people are frightened of spiders and sensitively ask the children to talk about their own feelings about these creatures. Try to allay any fears by providing lots of opportunities to observe and become familiar with spiders, and by reading spider stories, such as the traditional Anansi tales or *Charlotte's Web* by EB White (Puffin, 2010).
- **D&T** – Create webs by hammering nails into a wooden board and weaving thread in and out of them.

- Use printing techniques to create a collection of large spiders. Make a blob with a fist and then print four 'legs' on one side and four on the other using fingers. Cut around the spiders and mount them on string webs.
- Paint cut-down cardboard tubes black and attach pipe-cleaner legs. Put the spiders onto some netting suspended across a branch.
- Draw spiders' webs on card and then sew silver thread over the lines. Alternatively, sew or glue a circle of buttons to card to represent drops of dew. Wind the silver thread around the buttons and across to form the web threads. Attach tiny model spiders and flies, or make your own from fabric scraps.
- Create a large spider's web by pushing sticks into the ground to form a circle around a

create and display: Nature and the Environment

Chapter 4: **Natural Colours and Patterns**

Sunshine and Shadows

Sunshine Theatre

curtains · sun · wind · scenery · man · stage

'The sun and the wind'

We are exploring sunshine and shadows

Whole-class Starter

- Pass around a selection of hand and string puppets, as well as simple finger and stick puppets, and discuss how and why they are used. Explain that performing with puppets is an ancient worldwide means of passing on traditional tales.
- Read Aesop's fable 'The North Wind and the Sun', from *The Orchard Book of Aesop's Fables* by Michael Morpurgo and Emma Chichester Clark (Orchard, 2004) and one of the Brer Rabbit tales, 'The Moon in the Pond', from *The Adventures of Brer Rabbit and Friends* by Karima Amin, Joel Chandler Harris and Eric Copeland (DK Publishing, 2006).
- Suggest re-enacting these stories as puppet plays.

Focus of Learning
To build a traditional puppet theatre and puppets to re-enact traditional tales

Practical Activities

- Recall the two stories and discuss how one is set in bright sunshine and the other by moonlight. How will this affect the way that the children re-enact their stories?
- Suggest simplifying the activity by creating versatile stick puppets.
- Talk about the ancient tradition of shadow puppets and demonstrate this by holding the

create and display: **Nature and the Environment**

Chapter 4: **Natural Colours and Patterns**

black-card outline of a character between a shining torch and a white sheet to cast a shadow.
- Discuss the possibility of creating brightly coloured stick characters for 'The North Wind and the Sun' and atmospheric black shadow puppets for 'The Moon in the Pond'.
- Discuss how story performances take place in a theatre and talk about how a puppet theatre suitable for each story might look. The story set in sunshine could be in a theatre with rich curtains and a brightly coloured background. The shadow puppets for the night setting will need to be projected against a white background. The theatre could perhaps be a simple black outline of some curtains on a white sheet.
- Once the types of theatre have been decided, divide the groups into two sections and ask one to create 'daylight' theatres and the other to create 'moonlight' theatres. Encourage the children to consider which materials they will use and what sort of problems they think they might encounter. Suggest that they make notes and create diagrams showing their finished product.
- Provide materials for the children and be ready to support them with any problems as they work: for example, by demonstrating joining techniques or suggesting alternative materials.
- Once the theatres are made, provide the groups with copies of the stories so that they can decide how their characters will look and how to create them from suitable materials.
- Shadow puppets can be simple black-card outlines attached to sticks, whereas 'daytime' puppets can be created from card with collage materials attached and then fastened to sticks.
  - Suggest that they choose a narrator to read the words while others move the puppets. If necessary, shorten the story and divide it into manageable paragraphs.
    - Invite the groups to give performances of their plays to other children and parents.

Display Ideas

- Create a theatre on a display board by backing it in blue and hanging fabric in drapes at either side and along the top to represent the stage curtains.
- Create the effect of a stage along the bottom by attaching a strip of card or stiff hessian to each end and folding it in a curve so that it stands away from the board.
- Attach copies of the stick puppets for the daytime story to the blue background using a card hinge so that they stand away from the board but appear behind the strip of hessian representing the stage.
- Create labels for the characters.
- Place some of the shadow puppets around the display or mount them on a white-card screen to demonstrate the effect of light and shadow.
- Encourage the children to keep records of the development stages in the creation of their puppets and theatres in the form of photographs, diagrams, lists of materials and written notes.

Cross-curricular Links

- **Music** – Choose suitable music to play during performances: for example, rousing orchestral work when the wind blows wildly and peaceful dreamy music for the moonlight scenes.
- **Science** – Use the stories to motivate further work: for example, looking into the effects of extreme weather (the heat of the Sun and the force of the wind), and reflection (the Moon in the pond).

create and display: **Nature and the Environment**

Chapter 4: **Natural Colours and Patterns**

Day and Night

sun · light · sunlight · morning · midday · afternoon · breakfast · lunch

Day — bird, butterfly, caterpillar, ladybird, rabbit

Night — bat, stars, owl, badger, hedgehog

Whole-class Starter

- Set up an area with a small bed and items associated with bedtime routines, such as a cuddly toy, nightclothes, a clock, lamp and book. Enclose the area with a black drape to represent darkness.
- Play out night-time routines, such as cleaning teeth and getting washed and changed.
- Stay in the area to discuss what might be seen if the children went out for a walk in the moonlight. Would they see the same animals and hear the same noises as they would in the daytime? Would the sky look the same?

Focus of Learning

To explore differences between day and night
To learn language related to day and night and use these words in conversation

- Leave the children to follow their own ideas for related play.

Practical Activities

- Discuss night-time routines that help to make the children feel more comfortable when it is dark: for example, putting on a night light, an open door letting in light, or a happy story.
- Consider things that provide us with light

create and display: **Nature and the Environment**

Chapter 4: **Natural Colours and Patterns**

when we go out in the dark: for example, the Moon and stars, street lights and lights from windows. Create dark scenes in boxes, look through a hole in the side and then shine a torch through a hole in the lid to light them up. Talk about creatures who like to come out at night and show the children soft toys or models of these: for example, a hedgehog, owl and bat. Cut a hole in the side of a box with a lid, large enough for a child's hand. Put one of the toys inside and explain that there is a creature that only comes out at night hiding in the box. Take turns to put a hand through the hole and try to identify the creature using the sense of touch.

- Build a dark 'bedroom' from black drapes and ask some of the children to lie down and pretend to be asleep while others make the sounds of nocturnal creatures outside. Invite the 'sleeping' children to identify these using the sense of hearing.
- Ask the children to take photographs or make drawings and paintings depicting what they enjoy doing when they play outside during the day. Add appropriate captions.
- Talk about animals and birds that might be seen during the day and create individual pictures and models of them.
- Cut out and laminate some cards with different daily routines written on, such as 'I wake up', 'I eat my breakfast', to make a sequencing game involving arranging cards depicting daily routines in the order they occur.

Display Ideas

- Draw a large tree on a board and ask the children to draw season-specific things, such as leaves, blossom, birds and insects, adding extra items to the area surrounding the tree, for example flowers and rabbits on the grass and butterflies and birds in the sky.

- Ask the children to imagine what their finished tree would look like during the night. Would they still be able to see it clearly? Would the living creatures visiting it be the same?
- Create a 'night' version of the tree and ask the children to add what they think they might be able to see.
- Explain that you would like to show the two versions of the children's tree on one big display and ask for ideas about how to do this.
- Back one side of a display board light blue and the other dark blue, representing day and night. Create a large tree in the centre from padded black paper. Add a yellow collaged sun to one side and a silver moon to the other made in the same way.
- Provide the children with an exciting range of resources to embellish the daytime half of the tree. Encourage them to recreate the things that they drew during the initial discussion, for example birds with brightly coloured feathers.
- Replace the brightly coloured materials with dark materials to recreate the 'night' side.
- Create labels for the living things and surround the display with words associated with daily routines and the passing of time.
- Encourage the children to try this method to create individual images of a tree, folding the centre of the paper and adding things to either side. Display these together on a large board.

Cross-curricular Links

- **Creative Development** – Find ways of making dark places within sunny areas by creating shadows outdoors. Record these shadows by drawing around them with chalk or by taking photographs.
- **Mathematical Development** – Create a 'timeline' of daily routines using photographs along a display board.

create and display: Nature and the Environment

Chapter 4: Natural Colours and Patterns

Patterns in Nature

Focus of Learning
To explore natural patterns in the environment
To represent natural patterns using different media and creative techniques

Whole-class Starter

- Take the children outside on a breezy, sunny day with good cloud formation. Explain that they are going on a 'hunt for natural patterns'. Discuss the difference between 'natural' and 'man-made'.
- Let the children lie on the ground and look at the sky, having warned them that they should never look directly at the Sun. Talk about the patterns made by any clouds as they move across the sky. Now move under a tree and do the same. Discuss the patterns made by the leaves and branches and the changing light passing through them.
- Walk around searching for different examples of natural patterns: for example, the arrangement of petals on a flower, veins on a leaf, spots on a ladybird, or stripes on a caterpillar.
- Explain that the children are going to recreate these patterns, and talk about how they might remember them, perhaps by taking photographs or making sketches. Discuss the problems associated with this: for example, looking upwards while trying to draw, or constantly moving clouds or branches.
- Ask the children to record their favourite pattern using their chosen resource.

create and display: Nature and the Environment

Chapter 4: Natural Colours and Patterns

Practical Activities

- Provide a group of children with a safety mirror each and go for a 'sky walk', looking for cloud patterns in the mirror rather than looking directly at the sky. Discuss how much easier this is. Once the children have chosen a sky pattern they like, ask them to put the mirror down. Emphasise that they can choose what they would like in their picture – it could have branches and leaves or simply clouds. Talk about how this mirror image would look like a picture if it had a frame and discuss how to make one. Suggest creating a frame from something natural such as strips of wood and decorating it with found natural materials.

- Paint symmetrical pictures of butterflies by folding a sheet of paper in half, painting one half, and then folding it over and pressing down to print a mirror image on the other half.
- Create leaf patterns by cutting out identical leaves using contrasting coloured paper. Put a dark paper leaf on top of a lighter one and fold the two in half. Cut pieces out of the folded leaves from the centre fold, like making a paper snowflake. Unfold the two leaves and stick the dark leaf onto the lighter-coloured paper and the lighter leaf onto dark paper so that the background paper shows through the cut-out pieces. Cut the leaves out and stick them on a paper tree.
- Draw ladybirds and caterpillars with matching patterns on their backs.
- Create attractive paper flowers by cutting out petals in different colours and sticking them on top of one another in decreasing circles.
- Emphasise the rough textured pattern of the bark of a tree by creating rubbings using thick brown crayons.

Display Ideas

- Display the children's sky pictures *in situ* by leaving them on the ground and creating a 'viewing' trail from one to the other. Try putting vinyl flooring footprints on the ground to show viewers where to stand for the best vantage point. Discuss how the patterns in the frames are ever changing.
- Make use of intrusive classroom objects such as water pipes to hang indoor displays from. Thread some fabric onto a cane and drape over a pipe to display the children's natural patterns. Make a tree from brown paper padded from behind with newspaper. Attach the children's bark rubbings, leaf patterns and butterflies to this, and arrange their flowers along the base. Create a border of ladybirds and add appropriate labels and captions.

Cross-curricular Links

- **Maths** – Explore patterns in fruits and vegetables by cutting them in half. Print repeat patterns with them.
- **Literacy** – Think of words to describe natural patterns, such as 'whirls', 'stripes' and 'stipples', and include them in poems.

47

create and display: Nature and the Environment

Chapter 5: **Weather**

Sudden Showers

We covered an umbrella in tin foil and then went outside in the rain. We listened to hear the sounds that the rain created on the tin foil.

Whole-class Starter

- Invite the children to look out of the window while it is raining and describe how rain looks as it falls from the sky or runs down the glass.
- At the beginning of a week forecast to be wet, ask the children to bring in suitable waterproof clothing so they can go outside to run and splash around.
- Leave the children to follow their own ideas for a while before suggesting that they discover how rain feels on their open palms and upturned faces. Ask them to sniff and identify whether rain has any sort of smell.
- Bring out some umbrellas and suggest that the children stand still underneath them and listen to the sounds made by the raindrops. (These sounds can be amplified by covering the umbrellas with foil beforehand.)

Focus of Learning

To explore changes in the environment after sudden showers

To use appropriate vocabulary to describe how rain looks, sounds, smells and feels

Practical Activities

- Once the children return from their explorations in the rain, sit in a circle and discuss how being in the rain impacts on every sense. Write the words suggested by the children, such as 'sparkling', 'pitter-patter', 'damp', 'prickly' and 'silky',

create and display: Nature and the Environment

Chapter 5: Weather

and then decide which sense we use, for example, to know that rain is sparkling or that it makes a 'pitter-patter' sound.

- Provide the children with raindrop-shaped paper on which to write sentences that include their 'rain' words.
- Identify weather conditions associated with rain such as 'storm clouds', 'rainbows', 'showers', 'drizzle' and 'grey skies'. Type the children's words and mount them on shiny blue paper.
- Provide the children with small squares of card on which to paint pictures of these conditions and then use them on a weather chart or display about rain.
- Provide suitable paint and paper so that the children can mix shades of blue and grey and create large rain-inspired artwork.
- Invite the children to make rain patterns by dropping blobs of blue and grey paint onto paper and then holding the paper flat and carrying it out into the rain. Talk about the effect created as the raindrops land on the paper and run to make the colours mix.
- Create indoor rain showers by asking the children to wave or spatter a paintbrush over a large roll of paper to create drops and swirls. They can then cut out large and small raindrop shapes from the completed roll and stick them on pieces of paper to make their own rain shower pictures. (Save some raindrops for the main classroom display.)
- Cut out some raindrop shapes and invite the children to paint them blue and humanise them by adding quirky features such as lively smiles and tiny legs.

Display Ideas

- Back a display board with light-blue paper and add a contrasting dark-blue border.
- Mount an umbrella folded in half and covered in foil by stapling the folded half to the display board and surround this with the children's spatter-painted raindrops, 'lively' raindrops, typed 'rain' words and annotated raindrops.
- Stick the children's wet-weather pictures to the dark-blue paper to add interest to the border.

Cross-curricular Links

- **Personal, Social and Emotional Development** – Have fun splashing in puddles and making puddle pictures using large brushes to distribute the water.
- **Physical Development** – Pretend to be raindrops bouncing on the ground and rolling down hills, and recreate fine-drizzle patterns using fingers.

create and display: Nature and the Environment

Chapter 5: **Weather**

Sing a Rainbow

Whole-class Starter

- If you are lucky enough to see a rainbow through the window, take the children outside to observe it. Alternatively, create rainbows on the wall in the sunlight with glass prisms.
- Talk about how rainbows are formed by the Sun shining on raindrops. Make your own raindrops with a hosepipe on a sunny day and see if a rainbow appears.
- Identify the colours in a rainbow, demonstrating what 'indigo' looks like if necessary.

Focus of Learning

To explore weather conditions leading to the production of rainbows
To explore how primary colours can be mixed to create the colours of the rainbow

Practical Activities

- Provide the children with red, blue and yellow paint (the primary colours) and ask them to try to mix orange, green, indigo and violet, the other colours in a rainbow.

create and display: Nature and the Environment

Chapter 5: **Weather**

- Invite them to use these colours to paint their own rainbows, encouraging the use of sequencing words by asking questions such as: *What is the next colour?* and *Which colour comes after blue?* Hang up a large painting of a rainbow to refer to.
- Provide watery paint in the primary colours and paint a large red arch followed by an arch of yellow, overlapping the two colours slightly so that they merge. Discuss what happens when red merges with yellow. Continue adding watery layers of blue, then red, and watch as rainbow sequences appear.
- Blow bubbles in the sunlight and look for the swirling rainbow patterns on the surface.
- Ask the children what is meant by an 'arch' and talk about arches they have seen, for example on bridges and gates. Explain that 'bow' can be another word for a curve, similar to an arch, and discuss the meaning of 'rainbow'.
- Provide clay for the children to create arches or 'bow' shapes. Suggest that they form mini rainbows by pressing seven small bows together and painting them in the correct sequence of colours.
- Provide tissue in the colours of the rainbow so that the children can use them to create bows of colour and join them together.
- Use recycled and play materials, such as bottle tops, buttons, sweet wrappers, dolls' clothes and plastic bricks, and sort them into rainbow colours. Arrange them in adjacent bows to form floor rainbows.
- Make a huge balloon rainbow by attaching coloured balloons in a bow shape to a large display board.
- Provide pieces of canvas and invite groups of children to paint their own rainbows on them with thick paint. Embellish the rainbows with shiny items such as sequins and sparkly ribbon.
- Create rainbow beams of light by covering torches with coloured tissue and waving them in arches across white paper.

Display Ideas

- Back a display board with light-blue paper and cover this in raindrops made from blobs of dark-blue paint. Add a sun in one corner to shine on the raindrops.
- Create a border from raindrop shapes painted to match the colours of the rainbow and arranged on a strip of white paper in the correct sequence.
- Attach the children's clay rainbows at random, using PVA glue, with colour words between.
- Surround the display with examples of the children's rainbows created using different techniques, such as print, collage and paint merging.

Cross-curricular Links

- **Problem Solving, Reasoning and Numeracy** – Follow the sequence of colours in a rainbow to create patterns using print techniques, for example by printing arches with sponge circles.
- **Physical Development** – Create a huge outdoor rainbow using fabric, clothing and other items spread in arcs across the ground. Encourage stretching and bending movements, as well as fine delicate movements as you tweak the final rainbow shape.

create and display: **Nature and the Environment**

Chapter 6: Different Environments

Save the Rainforest

Focus of Learning
To raise the children's awareness of the need to protect the rainforests for the plants, wildlife and people that live there

Whole-class Starter

- Choose a fiction book with a strong message about protecting areas of the world that are under threat, for example *The Great Kapok Tree: A Tale of the Amazon Rain Forest* by Lynne Cherry (Voyager Books, 2000).
- Read the story and then discuss why the creatures who lived in the rainforest told the man who had come to fell a huge kapok tree about the important role the rainforest trees played in all of their lives.
- Discuss the ending of the story and what this tells us about the strength of the argument the creatures put forward to persuade the man to abandon his plan.

Practical Activities

- Set up a rainforest area in the corner of a room, enhancing it with cellophane creepers and lots of green cushions and drapes. Sit in this area to listen to stories and hold discussions.
- Provide creative materials so that the children can make animal masks. Suggest that they cover themselves in lengths of fabric in appropriate colours and put on the masks to dramatise *The Great Kapok Tree* and make up stories of their own with a similar message.

Chapter 6: Different Environments

- Encourage the children to take on the roles of animals and people living in the rainforest and ask them to answer questions in the hot seat about why their environment should be protected.
- Use bright paint, paper and collage materials to make individual and group pictures of rainforest creatures.
- Look carefully at images of the rainforest to find patterns: for example, the zigzag design of a snakeskin, the spirals and curls of creepers or the intricate veins on a leaf. Try to recreate these patterns using drawing or printing techniques.
- Invite the children to work in pairs to create posters encouraging people to 'Save our Rainforests'.

Display Ideas

- Suggest creating a display focusing on *The Great Kapok Tree* or another rainforest story you have shared. Use a long board and cover this in a drape of neutral fabric to represent the trunk of the tree. Adorn this with leaves in different shades of green drawn by the children.
- Talk about how the top of the rainforest is known as the 'canopy' and attach the children's pictures of wildlife, such as colourful parrots and lively monkeys, to this part of the tree. Recall how the area at the bottom of the tree is the 'understorey' and position more of their pictures, such as hissing snakes and prowling jaguars, here.
- Include pictures of the people in the story – the man with the axe and the child from the rainforest, for example.
- Create a caption to include the title of the featured book and a short blurb.
- Make additional displays, according to the work created by the children: for example, individual mounted pictures of wild creatures prowling in undergrowth made of green tissue, multicoloured birds hung as mobiles and an array of persuasive posters.

Cross-curricular Links

- **Music** – Create sound effects using instruments, everyday objects and voices and record these to add atmosphere during linked drama sessions.
- **D&T** – Make a display to include different design features such as flaps to hide menacing creatures, strings to hoist animals up and down the tree, and ribbon creepers for monkeys to swing on.

create and display: Nature and the Environment

Chapter 6: **Different Environments**

Mountains

Whole-class Starter

- Invite the children to bring in images of mountains, such as photographs, magazine pictures or web images. Ask individuals to describe their images.
- Create a list of the features that all of these mountains share, and then identify aspects that are different: for example, they may be snow-capped, formed from steep jagged rocks or covered by forests.
- Discuss the difference between a hill and a mountain, and what is meant by a 'chain of mountains' or a 'mountain range'.

Practical Activities

- Divide the class into groups to conduct further research into mountains. Provide each group

Focus of Learning

To discover more about mountains and represent this knowledge using creative techniques

with a mountain-related question to answer using books and computers: for example, *What are mountains made from? What do mountains look like? Where are mountains found? What is a mountain range? What is a volcano? Where is the world's highest mountain and what is it called? Where is the highest mountain in Great Britain and what is it called?*

54

create and display: Nature and the Environment

Chapter 6: Different Environments

- Ensure that the children have access to writing materials, computers and printers to present their answers using their chosen media. Bring the class together to share their findings.
- Make models of mountains using a range of different creative media, such as scrunched-up newspaper and paint, sand, clay or commercially produced modelling materials. Encourage the children to consider scale if they plan to introduce trees and small figures onto their mountains.

Display Ideas

- Create a large mountain display, deciding together which features the mountain will have: for example, will it be snow-capped, have trees on the slopes, a lake at the bottom?
- Back a large board in blue to represent the sky and then pad out the shapes of the mountain by stapling scrunched-up newspaper to the backing. Staple paper or fabric around the edges of the newspaper to create a 3D mountain. Add features such as streams and waterfalls created from collage materials. If the mountain is to be snow-capped, talk about how this will be represented: for example, using a mixture of white paint and PVA glue sprinkled with silver glitter, or by sticking pieces of white sheeting or tissue to the finished mountain.
- Encourage the children to think about how they will represent additional features that might be seen on their chosen mountain, such as forests, ski lifts, climbers, walkers, animals, chalets and so on. Provide appropriate materials for this so that they can complete and add them to finish the display.
- In discussion with the children, add appropriate captions and labels: for example, facts that they discovered in their earlier group research into mountains.
- Create a border: for example, using printed fir trees, or mini mountains printed along paper strips to give a mountain range effect.
- Drape a nearby table with appropriate green, brown or white fabric for displaying the children's mountain models.
- Take photographs during the making of the display and models so that you can create a 'step-by-step' display showing the process from start to finish. Add the children's own comments, as well as links to the learning taking place, to encourage parents to share the display and understand how much the children gained from this project.

Cross-curricular Links

- **Science** – Make your own erupting volcanoes by surrounding a small plastic bottle with clay to form a volcano shape, with the top of the bottle emerging from the clay. Add warm water mixed with red food colouring to the bottle. Put in a few drops of washing-up liquid and two large spoons of baking soda. Slowly add vinegar and stand back!
- **Drama** – Set up a role-play camp on an imaginary mountain, dress as mountaineers and dramatise imaginary scenarios.

create and display: Nature and the Environment

Chapter 6: **Different Environments**

Deserts

Whole-class Starter

- Explore resources associated with deserts, such as images and models of desert creatures.
- Join the children at play in a role-play desert set in a sand tray and maximise learning opportunities by planning further activities around their interests: for example, encourage children who are fascinated by the 'creepy-crawly' scorpions they find hiding under logs in the sand to search books and websites to discover more about them.

Focus of Learning

To compare a local environment with a desert environment

To represent a desert using creative media

Practical Activities

- Show the children a cactus plant in a pot. Point out the sharp prickles and emphasise that they should look rather than touch.

56

create and display: Nature and the Environment

Chapter 6: Different Environments

- Make comparisons between the plants from outdoors with their juicy green leaves and the cactus with dry spines.
- Introduce the word 'desert' and explain that many cacti grow there. Establish what the children already know about deserts.
- Recall the conditions needed for plants to grow, explaining that deserts are very hot and dry, so the plants that grow there have little water. Cactus plants are able to retain water because they have sharp spines instead of flat leaves. These also protect them from being eaten by desert creatures.
- Have fun making cactus plants from green dough and sticking blunted cocktail stick 'spines' all over the surface.
- Present the children with a selection of models from a desert environment, such as scorpions, snakes and lizards. Discuss differences between desert creatures and 'local' animals. Take the desert creatures to a sand tray filled with a layer of dry sand. 
- Satisfy the curiosity of those who are asking lots of questions about the lifestyle of the desert creatures in the sand tray – for example: *Where will they sleep? What will they eat? Where will they hide from danger?* – by exploring books and/or the internet.

Display Ideas

- Create a desert display behind the sand tray, defining the area with blue drapes to represent the sky and hessian for the sand.
- Staple a huge fabric sun to the sky drapes.
- Decide together on additional detail to include, for example a huge lizard, cactus plants and snakes.
- Bubble wrap has an ideal texture for a lizard's rough skin and can be painted in green and gold, provided the paint is mixed with PVA glue first.
- Huge cactus plants can be produced using card, green paint and blunted cocktail sticks.
- Take photographs as the children are working and write down their comments. Display the photographs along with captions that include the children's words.
- Ask the children to think of interesting 'desert' words to add to the display – for example, 'scratchy', 'dusty', 'warm' and 'sizzle' – and attach these in appropriate positions.
- Finally, decide upon a title for the display (the children who created the display featured on these pages chose 'We Like Lizards!' to sum up the main focus of their desert experience).

Cross-curricular Links

- **Problem Solving, Reasoning and Numeracy** – Encourage the children to make up related counting songs: for example, 'Five scuttling scorpions went out one day, over the sand and far away' (to the tune 'Five Little Ducks').
- **Communication, Language and Literacy** – Make up and dramatise stories about the desert creatures while playing in the sandpit.

create and display: Nature and the Environment

Chapter 6: Different Environments

Cold Lands – the Poles

[Display board showing Arctic and Antarctic regions with labels: North Pole, Arctic, seal, orca, The Inuit people live in the Arctic, igloo, Eskimo, The Arctic and Antarctic are in the polar regions, Inuit, walrus, arctic fox, The Polar regions are icy areas around the North and South Pole, Polar bears live in the Arctic, In the winter the sun never rises, In the summer the sun never sets, polar bear, arctic tern, penguin, Penguins live Antarctic, Antarctic, South Pole]

Whole-class Starter

- Show the children models or pictures of animals that live in the Arctic or Antarctic: for example, polar bears, penguins, Arctic foxes, walruses and Arctic terns. Ask them to name those that they can, and introduce the names of those that are unfamiliar.
- Show the children a globe and identify the North and South Poles. Introduce the terms 'Arctic' and 'Antarctic' and point out these areas. Explain that the creatures they have been naming live in these cold lands – some, such as polar bears and Arctic foxes, in the Arctic and others, such as penguins, in the Antarctic.
- Talk about the climate in these areas, explaining that it is always very cold. Describe how the Sun never sets in the summer and never rises in the winter. Make comparisons with the climate that the children are familiar with.

Focus of Learning
To discover more about the cold lands of the world

- Introduce the word 'Inuit' and explore images of these people. Talk about how they dress, what they eat and where they live, pointing out that today they live in homes made from a variety of materials but still build igloos for shelter, for example when out hunting.

Practical Activities

- Set up an activity to reinforce awareness of the appearance

create and display: **Nature and the Environment**

Chapter 6: Different Environments

and lifestyle of creatures living in cold lands.
- Invite the children to work in pairs to find out key facts about one of the creatures they have been discussing as a class. Provide access to suitable books and websites. Ask each pair to write these facts on a large speech bubble.
- Laminate images of the featured creatures and create matching silhouettes. Display the silhouettes on a board and run a ribbon from each one to the corresponding image. Attach the children's completed speech bubbles to the mouths of the corresponding creatures.
- The children can then read the speech bubbles, guess which creature is described and check whether they have guessed correctly by following the ribbon from the silhouette to the laminated image.
- Set up a role-play area to represent the North Pole, screening off a corner using white fabric draped over free-standing screens bordered by corrugated card to represent icicles. Hang thin, shimmering, blue fabric from the ceiling to enclose the screens and decorate the whole area with 'cold' items such as silver stars and images of snowy landscapes. Introduce soft toy animals such as polar bears, appropriate books, white cushions and rugs. Stand a pop-up igloo/tent draped in white sheeting next to the screens. Encourage the children to make up scenarios linked to the theme: for example, going on a fishing expedition involving sinking holes in the ice.

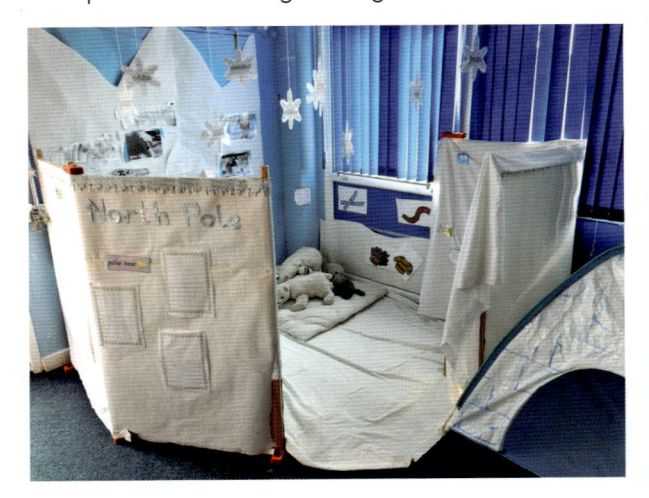

Display Ideas

- Create a display representing the Arctic and Antarctic. Invite some children to help to back a large board in blue to represent the oceans and cut out two large white land masses to attach to the top and bottom of the board. Label them 'Arctic' and 'Antarctic'.
- Place a blue circle in the centre of the display, with the four compass points indicated. Add a signpost with arrows pointing to the North and South Poles.
- Decide together which creatures will inhabit the two land masses and create these from collage materials. Create some Inuit families and igloos for them to shelter in.
- Attach the people and animals in the empty spaces at either side of the board.
- Fill in remaining spaces with collage icebergs, textured blue collage materials and fact captions. Label the children's collages and paintings of people and animals.
- Create a border: for example, with white strips of border roll covered in scrunched-up white-tissue snowballs and silver snowflakes.
- Add a suitable title, such as 'Cold Lands', made from white card letters sprinkled with glitter to create a sparkle effect.
- Make additional displays, according to the interests of the children: for example, focus on polar bears and include the children's paintings, printed images and fact captions.
- Create an appropriate 'cold lands' atmosphere to the classroom by making a large polar bear head and two paws to hang over the door to greet visitors.

Cross-curricular Links

- **D&T** – Add interest to the display with working models: for example, a card penguin threaded on a loop of string stretching from the Arctic at the top of the board to the Antarctic at the bottom. By pulling this string the penguin can be raised and lowered so that the children can move it to the correct habitat.
- **Art and Design** – Create individual representations of the people and animals, and features such as icebergs and igloos, using collage techniques.

create and display: Nature and the Environment

59

Chapter 6: Different Environments

Cold Lands – Arctic Tundra

Whole-class Starter

- Ask the children to identify the North Pole on a globe. Introduce the term 'Arctic tundra' and explain that this covers a vast area in the far northern hemisphere.
- Talk about what the climate might be like and how the landscape might look. Ask questions about the types of animals and plants that might be able to survive there.

Practical Activities

- Engage the children's interest by introducing some unusual facts about tundra vegetation. Explain that 'tundra' means 'barren or treeless land' and that it is a unique area with distinct living things that have adapted to survive in this harsh climate. Explain that this frozen land is covered with a thin layer of soil called permafrost that supports the unusual plant life in summer.

Focus of Learning
To extend work on cold lands by focusing on a specific ecosystem

- Look at some actual examples or images of bush and ground-hugging lichen, and short plants such as cotton grass. Ask the children to draw pastel pictures of how they imagine this barren land to look.

create and display: Nature and the Environment

Chapter 6: **Different Environments**

- Discuss the harsh conditions the animals have to endure and how they manage to survive: for example, some change colour for protection or develop thicker fur, such as the Arctic fox and polar bear. Others hibernate during the coldest months.
- Provide a selection of clothes and resources, some suitable for a tundra expedition and others for a beach holiday. Ask the children to discuss how they could use the given resources to protect themselves if they were visiting this climate in the winter. Suggest that they dress one group member appropriately and then talk the class through their reasoning.
- Recall previous research into animals that live in cold lands (pages 58–59) and ask the children to name some of them. Introduce any unfamiliar ones and remember to include those that live up in the mountains, such as mountain goats, elk and sheep.
- Identify which ones live exclusively in the Arctic or Antarctic in order to decide which ones might live in the Arctic tundra.
- Ask the children to make a list of animals living in the Arctic tundra using books and the internet.
- Invite the children to work in pairs to find key facts about one of the creatures on the list. Ask each pair to write these facts on a square of paper and stick the paper on card to create a 'lift-the-flap' fact card for others to read.

Display Ideas

- Suggest creating a display representing the differences in the Arctic tundra in spring, summer and winter.
- Divide a large board into three sections with a wide border between each. Back the spring and summer sections in blue and the winter in black. Create the landscape for each section using coloured paper and adding vegetation with collage techniques.
- Invite the children to create animals that live in the Arctic tundra using collage materials. Attach them to the appropriate landscape.
- Emphasise seasonal changes in temperature by asking the children to draw and cut out two thermometers showing the temperature in winter and summer.
- Create a title for each section and label the individual animals.
- Attach the children's 'lift-the-flap' fact cards in the wide sections between each large image.
- Make snowshoes from bent sticks and string, and display them with captions.
- Encourage the children to make ice sculptures using polystyrene pieces, add glitter and display on a table top with some fairy lights and shiny cloth for effect.

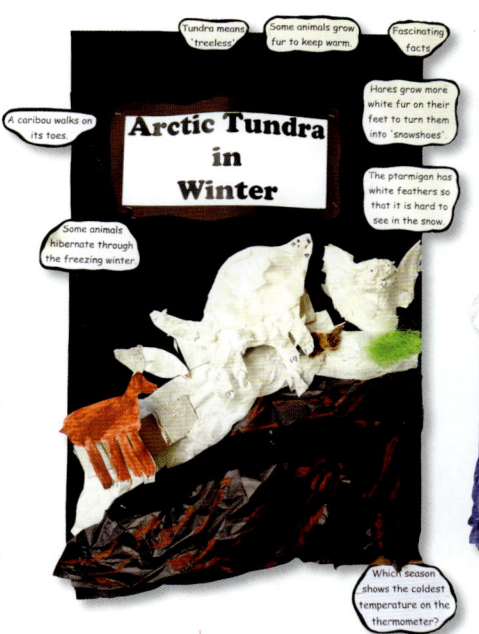

Cross-curricular Links

- **Literacy** – Work in pairs to research and represent information discovered about the creatures that live in the Arctic tundra with 'lift-the-flap' cards.
- **Art and Design** – Create individual representations of tundra animals using collage techniques.

create and display: **Nature and the Environment**

Chapter 7: Energy

Fossil Fuels

Fossil fuels form underground when organic material decays over a long time.

Fossil fuels are oil, gas and coal.

Most of our energy is generated by burning fossil fuels.

fish
seaweed
sand
gas pocket
fern

Some fuel is burned directly.

Some fuel is used in power stations to produce electricity.

sea
starfish
fossil
oil layer

We need to save energy to make fossil fuels last longer.

We need to find new ways to produce power because fossil fuel supplies are running out.

Whole-class Starter

- Provide a range of both plant and animal fossils for the children to explore before asking individuals to choose one to describe. Establish how fossils are formed, beginning with the children's existing understanding of the process and extending this by filling any 'missing links' in their knowledge.
- Introduce the word 'fuel' and ask the children what they know about the meaning of this word. Again extend information.
- Put the two words you have been discussing together and ask for suggestions about what 'fossil fuels' might be.
- Establish the children's awareness of gas, oil and coal and explain that they are all fossil fuels.

Practical Activities

- Explain how fossil fuels are formed over a long period of time and demonstrate this practically

Focus of Learning
To understand what is meant by a 'fossil fuel' and the need to find alternative sustainable energy sources

by putting some flowers or leaves on a flat board, covering them with another and then adding layers of heavy magazines and catalogues to represent the enormous force on the decaying matter from silted debris above. Leave, and check over time to see what is happening to the flowers and leaves underneath.

create and display: Nature and the Environment

Chapter 7: **Energy**

drilling for natural gas. Follow this by explaining with the aid of images what happens to these fuels: for example, coal is transformed into electricity in a power station and travels through cables to homes and factories. Suggest representing this as a model using recycled resources.

Display Ideas

- Invite some of the children to help to back a large board in a suitable colour for displaying their work. Fasten the children's three pictorial representations of subterranean coal, gas and oil onto the display. Discuss with each group how they might annotate their picture so that others can understand exactly what is happening: for example, by using art straws to form arrows representing the pressure on the decaying materials and adding labels and captions.
- Create a border from thin white fabric or paper clouds swirling around the whole display.
- Drape a shelf or table with black fabric and use this to display the children's models: for example, a power station at one end and a house at the other joined to art-straw 'pylons' with string cables.
- Add related artefacts as space allows, such as fossils, coal nuggets and an oil can.

Cross-curricular Links

- **PSHCE** – Consider the long-term effects of using fossil fuels on our environment and discuss how we can make responsible choices using renewable energy.

- In groups, represent this by drawing three cross sections of earth, one with a layer of coal created from black crayon, another a pocket of gas coloured grey, and another a pocket of oil coloured brown/green.
- Invite the groups to make larger pictorial representations of how each of the three fossil fuels are formed. Discuss how these might vary: for example, coal will be below land made from decaying ferns and trees, whereas oil and gas might be under the sea and contain fossil shells and sea creatures.
- Provide large sheets of paper as the base and a wide range of collage materials and paints to build up the picture. Join groups to discuss how they plan to represent the layers and the seam or pocket of fuel. Encourage them to consider how they will differentiate between the living plants and creatures above ground and the fossil materials below.
- Having established where and how the fossil fuels are formed, discuss how they can be reached and brought to the surface. Show images of oil rigs, coal mines and machines

create and display: **Nature and the Environment**

63

Chapter 7: **Energy**

Wind Power

Whole-class Starter

- Take the children out on a windy day and ask them how it feels to have the wind blowing in their faces and against their bodies. Now ask them to run and discuss whether it is easier to run into the wind or in the same direction.
- Look around for evidence of the action of the wind, for example leaves swirling on the ground, flags flying, washing billowing on a line and branches bending and swaying.

Practical Activities

- Ask the children if they can think of ways that the wind can be useful, for example drying washing or flying a kite. Go outdoors and set up practical demonstrations of both.
- Ask if the children have ever seen a real windmill and talk about how they work by harnessing the power of the wind to turn the millstone and grind the flour.

Focus of Learning
To understand how the wind acts as a force to move objects in different directions

create and display: **Nature and the Environment**

Chapter 7: Energy

- Create some paper windmills and try them outdoors. Make a working model of a windmill using card for the sails and a cardboard tube for the structure. 
- Link this to wind turbines the children may have seen. Discuss the importance of harnessing this energy source.
- Decide whether heavy or light items are more likely to blow in the wind by observing things that stay still despite the force of the wind. Ask the children if the wind is always helpful. Show them images of hurricanes and tornadoes to demonstrate that the wind can be a destructive force.
- Create wind chimes by attaching metal objects with string to coat hangers. Suspend them outdoors and listen to changes in sound as the wind gathers and reduces force.
- Take the children outdoors and ask them which way they think the wind is blowing. Demonstrate how to verify their answer using the 'wet finger' test, holding a dampened finger in the air and then deciding which side is coldest. Make a simple windsock or weathervane so that the changes in direction of the wind can be observed. Use a compass to mark the four compass points in chalk on the playground and stand a large plant pot full of soil in the centre, then push a streamer on a stick securely into the pot.
- Create simple parachutes from a square of fabric attached by string from the corners to a small model figure. Throw the parachute in the air and watch it move as it falls.
- Experiment with making paper aeroplanes, balsa-wood gliders and flags to fly in the wind.
- Create your own wind using folded paper fans and waft tiny boats across a water tray.

Display Ideas

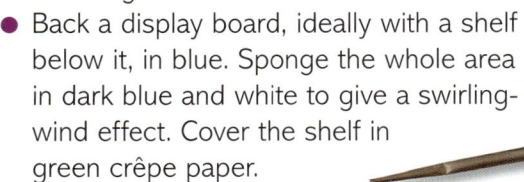

- Invite the children to create a display illustrating the busy mayhem of a windy day. Talk about things that might be included, such as children flying paper windmills and a line of washing billowing in the breeze. 
- Back a display board, ideally with a shelf below it, in blue. Sponge the whole area in dark blue and white to give a swirling-wind effect. Cover the shelf in green crêpe paper.
- Ask the children to paint pictures of themselves in a suitable size to fit behind a painted corrugated cardboard fence at the base of the display. Attach the fence at each end and curve it outwards so that it stands out from the board.
- Cut out the children's paintings of themselves and stick them to the back of the fence.
- Attach the children's paper windmills to the hands of the painted characters.
- Invite other children to draw items of clothing and cut them out. Attach a washing line from one side of the display to the other and hang these clothes on it using small pegs.
- Print some 'wind' words and attach these to the display along with the title 'Windy Days'.
- Create a border of 'clouds' made from crumpled white tissue.

Cross-curricular Links

- **D&T** – Make working models of windmills and turbines.
- **Maths** – Develop measuring skills when making windmills, paper aeroplanes and fans.

create and display: Nature and the Environment

Chapter 8: Art Exhibition

Art Exhibition

Creating an art exhibition is a way of transforming the learning environment of part of your school into a positive, vibrant place to display children's artwork. This can often be done in parts of the school which tend to be dull and ignored, such as corridors. This can be taken a step further by inviting parents and children to art shows at your 'gallery' – parents evening is the perfect time for this!

Explosion of Feet

The Reggio Emilia approach stems from the belief that children's early development provides strong building blocks for the unique individuals they will become. As the name suggests, it began in the Reggio Emilia district of Italy where parents, supported by the primary school teacher Loris Magaluzzi (1920–1994), created opportunities for children to follow their own pathways to learning through practical exploration of the world around them. This display encourages children to explore form, shape and colour using their bodies as part of the creative process.

Resources

- Paint in a variety of colours
- Sheets of white paper large enough to create a floor-to-ceiling display
- Shallow dishes for paint
- Bowls of soapy water for washing, and paper towels

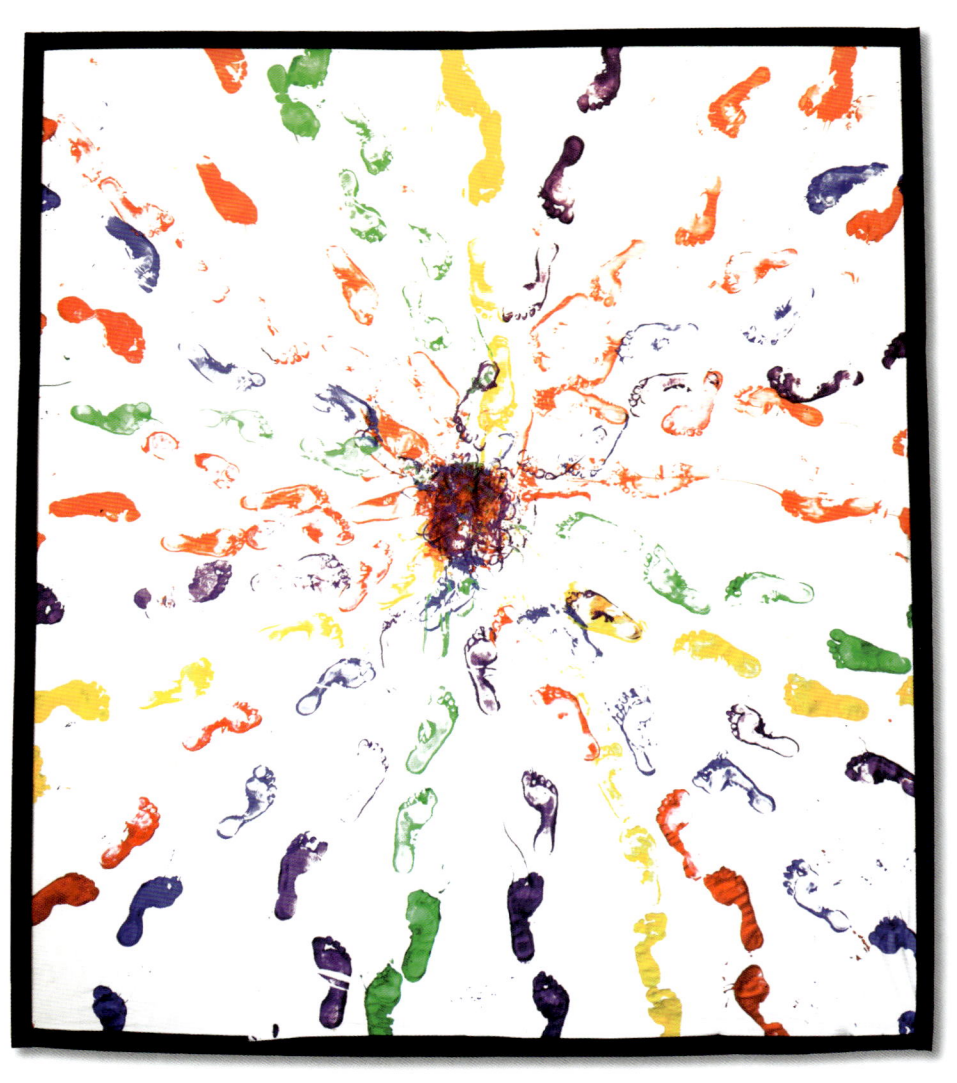

Approach

- Provide children with the paper and paint without paintbrushes so that they can experiment with making coloured marks on paper without the aid of tools.
- Ensure that washing facilities are to hand: for example, putting bowls of soapy water and paper towels on the floor next to chairs for washing feet.
- Create a group picture using the techniques the children have adopted: for example, hand and foot prints or finger painting.
- Encourage the children to explore their developing ideas, such as making a rainbow from handprints or an explosion of colour from footprints.

create and display: Nature and the Environment

Chapter 8: **Art Exhibition**

Pop Art

Pop art emerged in the 1950s when British and American artists began to observe the cultural icons of the era prevalent in advertising, television, films and comic books. They represented these icons through different art techniques to portray the changing attitudes of 1960s society. Good examples of pop artists are Andy Warhol (1928–1987), who often experimented with repeat images of everyday objects and famous faces of the time, capturing the same image in different colours, and Roy Lichtenstein (1923–1997), whose interest lay in comic books. He created detailed paintings in comic-book form, complete with speech bubbles.

Resources

- Examples of pop art images by artists such as Andy Warhol and Roy Lichtenstein
- Brightly coloured pens and paint
- Paper and brushes
- Bright backing paper and contrasting borders
- Examples of comic books and magazines with pop culture advertisements

Approach

- Explore the images and encourage the children to talk about what they like or dislike about them.
- Discuss how everyday items from our popular culture, such as drink cans and faces of famous people, are presented in different colours against contrasting backgrounds, often as repeat images.
- Make links between the work of famous pop artists in the discussed examples and the artwork in comic books and magazine advertisements.
- Provide materials and invite the children to become 'pop artists', creating their own pictures, comic strips and advertisements employing repeat images of objects representative of today's popular culture.
- Display individual work against an eye-catching coloured background with a contrasting border.

67

create and display: **Nature and the Environment**

Chapter 8: **Art Exhibition**

Line and Colour

This display encourages children to appreciate shape, form and colour in the natural world and to represent these using art techniques.

Resources

- Snails or images of snails
- Shallow dishes
- Paint and brushes
- Marbles
- Felt pens
- Coloured and white paper

Approach

- Observe snails as they leave their silvery trails and discuss the paths they take. Talk about whether they always move in straight or curved lines, or whether this varies. Suggest representing these tracks as colourful designs.
- Invite the children to take a pen on a snail's trail around a piece of paper, encouraging them to do this at random so that the trail crosses over itself. Look at the design created and suggest filling in the sections enclosed by the trail with blocks of colour so that no enclosure lacks colour.
- Discuss the snail trails they have just created. Is a snail's trail really a clean line resembling the one they have just drawn or does it lack defined edges?
- Put a piece of coloured paper in a shallow dish, dip a marble in some thick paint in a contrasting colour and roll it around over the paper to create another version of a snail trail. Repeat with marbles dipped in different colours to create an attractive design.
- Compare the two designs and discuss preferences.
- Mount the pictures together on a black background.

create and display: Nature and the Environment

Chapter 8: Art Exhibition

Aztec Shields

The Aztec army carried shields to fend off arrows and spears. These shields were made of natural materials such as woven reeds, with feathers lining the outside. The designs on the covers were frequently geometric. Sometimes they included figures of the animals that represented the different strengths that the Aztecs believed they received from them. The adorning feathers also varied in colour, type and design according to the owner's status and merit.

Resources

- Images of Aztec shields showing a range of designs
- Images of family coats of arms
- Paint and brushes
- Felt pens
- Collage materials such as tissue and foil
- Thick tape
- Thick card

Approach

- Discuss the protective purpose of a shield and talk about the sort of weapons the Aztecs would have needed to protect themselves from.
- Explore the shape of the shields and the designs on them. Ask the children to choose one that they particularly like and then say why.
- Explain how the shield design would often identify the rank of the person and look at some images of coats of arms. Discuss what these designs might signify.
- Invite the children to create Aztec shields adorned with their own designs. Provide them with card and paint, and drawing and collage materials. Talk about how they will make the shield circular and discuss how to protect the edges from fraying with strong tape.
- Display the children's shields on a bright background for maximum effect.
- Extend this activity to involve designing family coats of arms.

create and display: Nature and the Environment

Chapter 8: Art Exhibition

Circles of Colour

Wassily Kandinsky (1866–1944) was a Russian artist who was especially interested in colour. He used colour to show emotion and encourage others to feel emotion. As his work became more abstract he began painting patches of colour instead of objects.

Resources

- Images of work by Kandinsky, such as his coloured concentric circles
- Paint in the primary colours and white
- Brushes
- White card

Approach

- Explore images of Kandinsky's colour studies and explain how he wanted to show how he was feeling through colour.
- Talk about how certain colours reflect how we feel, for example calm, frightened or angry. Try looking at shades of colour and discuss whether they have the same effect: for example, red might link to angry feelings but pink might make us calmer.
- Invite the children to mix different colours using the three primary colours.
- Create shades of a colour by adding white to a primary colour.
- Suggest that the children paint circles of different shades of the same colour to produce their own colour designs.
- Try creating designs employing a range of colours including black.
- Talk about how the designs make us feel and think of titles that reflect these feelings, such as 'Red Rage'.
- Mount the pictures and display them on a strong primary colour.

create and display: Nature and the Environment

Chapter 8: Art Exhibition

Natural Silhouettes

Silhouettes of trees and animals can provide stark contrast to a beautiful sunset or a sky glowing with rainbow colours, emphasising their line and form. Use previous work on shadow puppetry (pages 42–43) as a springboard to inspire the children to experiment with artwork involving the creation of silhouettes against a rich background of colour.

Resources

- Shadow puppets and a light source
- Photographic images with silhouettes of animals and plants in the foreground, for example African sunsets
- Paper, pastels and black crayons

Approach

- Recall shadow puppet work and discuss the effect of the strong black image against the light background. Talk about how the outline of the puppet stands out in sharp detail.
- Explore photographic images of the natural world where animals and plants appear in detail as silhouettes against a strong sunset.
- Invite the children to create their own sunset pictures using pastels and then add animal, tree and plant silhouettes in the foreground with black crayon. Talk about which creatures might be the most effective on the picture because of their distinctive outlines, for example bats and elephants. Decide whether trees should be bare so that branches stand out clearly, or filled with leaves, which might make the silhouette less effective.
- Discuss the contrast of the strong colour and black outlines when they are side by side in one image.
- Experiment with using black paper instead of crayon to create the silhouettes.
- Mount the children's artwork in groups of four against a plain background, or frame them individually to hang in a row.

Cross-curricular Links

- **Music** – Find suitable pieces of music to link with the displays in your art exhibition. Play these in the background as visitors are enjoying the artwork: for example, Beethoven's *Pastoral Symphony* to link with displays with a country theme, *Danse Macabre* by Saint-Saëns for atmospheric silhouette images, or *Mars* from *The Planets Suite* by Gustav Holst for the Aztec warriors.
- **Literacy** – Invite a group of children to design and print an exhibition leaflet with blurb about the artists and techniques as well as photographs and descriptions of the displays. Leave a visitors' book alongside the leaflets in the area so that children and adults can find out more about the work on display and write comments about the exhibition.

create and display: Nature and the Environment

SCHOLASTIC

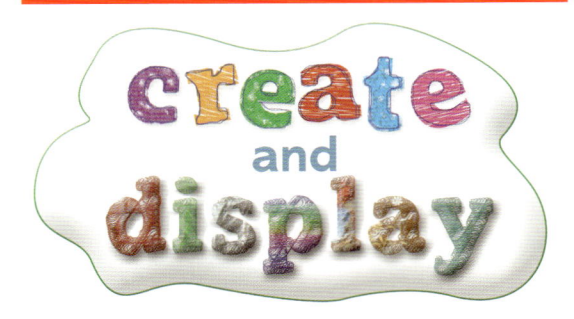

create and display

Titles in this series:

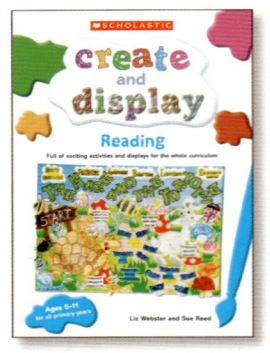

ISBN: 978-1407-11915-1 (Reading)

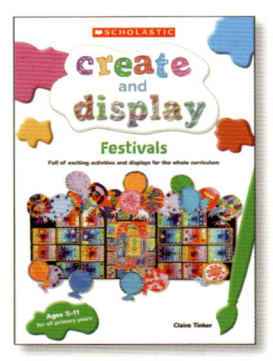

SBN: 978-1407-11918-2 (Festivals)

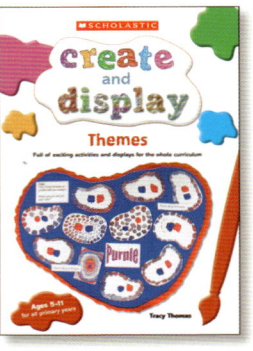

ISBN: 978-1407-11916-8 (Themes)

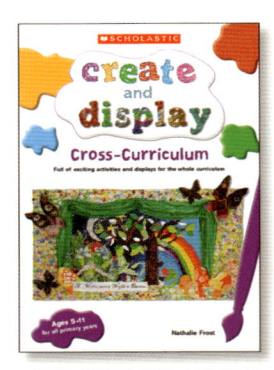

ISBN: 978-1407-11917-5 (Cross-Curriculum)

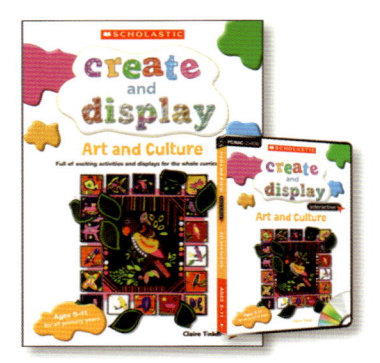

ISBN: 978-1407-12527-5 (Book)
ISBN: 978-1407-12533-6 (CD-ROM)
(Art and Culture)

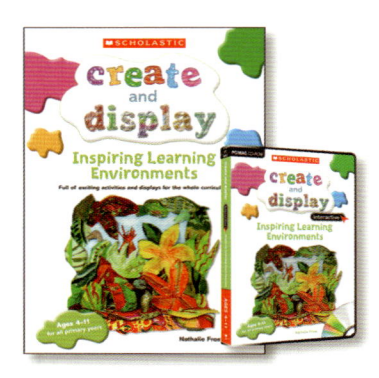

ISBN: 978-1407-12526-8 (Book)
ISBN: 978-1407-12532-9 (CD-ROM)
(Inspiring Learning Environments)

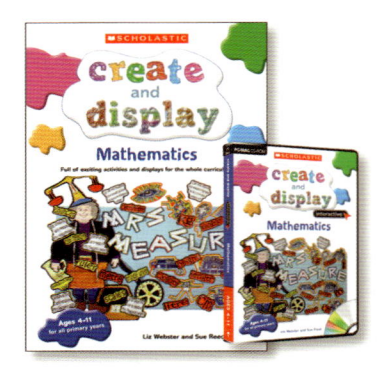

ISBN: 978-1407-12525-1 (Book)
ISBN: 978-1407-12531-2 (CD-ROM)
(Mathematics)

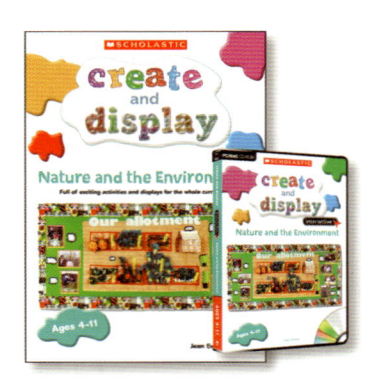

ISBN: 978-1407-12528-2 (Book)
ISBN: 978-1407-12534-3 (CD-ROM)
(Nature and the Environment)

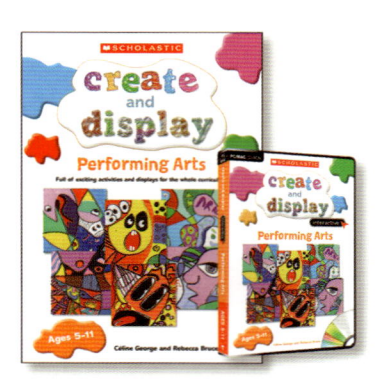

ISBN: 978-1407-12530-5 (Book)
ISBN: 978-1407-12536-7 (CD-ROM)
(Performing Arts)

ISBN: 978-1407-12529-9 (Book)
ISBN: 978-1407-12535-0 (CD-ROM)
(Science)

To find out more, call: **0845 603 9091**
or visit our website **www.scholastic.co.uk**